USE YOUR
IMAGINATION

EARTH GODS

Demeter (Ceres)	Dionysus (Bacchus)
corn and growth	the vine, wine

MINOR GODS

Eros (Cupid)	Hymen	Hebe	Iris
love	marriage	youth	rainbow

NINE MUSES

Clio (history); Urania (astronomy); Melpomene (tragedy); Thalia (comedy); Terpsichore (dance); Calliope (epic poetry); Erato (love poetry); Polyhymnia (songs to gods); Euterpe (lyric poetry).

THREE GRACES

Aglaia (Splendour); Euphrosyne (Mirth); Thalia (Pleasure).

USE YOUR IMAGINATION

An introduction, through mythology, to literature, creative writing and general studies

HUGH McKAY
P. R. SMART

JOHN MURRAY
50 Albemarle Street   London

First Published in Great Britain 1973

First published in Australasia and S.E. Asia in 1969 by
A. H. & A. W. REED
Now published by
Longman Paul Limited
Auckland, New Zealand

Printed in Hong Kong by Wing Tai Cheung Printing Co. Ltd.

0 7195 2819 4

CONTENTS

MAN AND HIS ENVIRONMENT

LIST OF ILLUSTRATIONS

PREFACE

Teachers who expect a text to be stimulating, a fruitful source of exercises and a guide in unfamiliar fields will find that Mr McKay and Mr Smart have met all their requirements; for the extracts are good, and the questions are practical, numerous, and varied enough to allow teachers to select what is useful for their purposes.

Imagination is the unifying factor of the book. It links the myths with later literature and, by grouping under topics, leads to related creative, or imaginative, writing by pupils. It is easy to say, "Write an essay on Fire." It is far more profitable to say, "Here is what others have written. Think about these questions; let your imagination work on this material and see what you can do."

There are good reasons for starting with myths. They are interesting for their own sake. They are useful for their allusions and for the introduction of themes which appear in later literature. Through the associated questions they show widely separated peoples in a common search for standards as relevant now, as then, because they deal with human qualities and human relationships.

The myths and the extracts are especially suitable for pupils between twelve and fourteen years of age. The wide range of ability and attainment at this stage should present no problems. There is substantial variation in reading levels and in difficulty of discussion questions. The creative writing topics, however, can be handled by any class at its particular level.

Although there is an association with the *Let's Learn English* course, this book could be used to advantage with any of the texts currently used for the twelve to fourteen age-group, as an introduction to wider reading and as a source book for general studies and creative writing.

M. K. Denholm
Nelson College

ACKNOWLEDGMENTS

Most teachers quickly accumulate large collections of teaching material. One field, however, which I found deficient in readily-available classroom material, was that of mythology. I was fortunate in that I had a Head of Department, Mr M. K. Denholm, who encouraged me to look further afield and later to consider publishing my growing collection of extracts. He has helped me greatly at all stages of this book. At this time I became associated with my collaborator, Peter Smart, and he has helped me with the design of the book and has contributed much of the teaching material. I was also fortunate in being able to call upon the interest and experience of Mr I. J. Major, Mr J. F. Wheeler, Mr L. T. Elphick, and Mr J. W. Russell, fellow members of staff; and of Dr J. V. Nicholas, who gave me many useful suggestions as well as the article on atomic energy; and Tim Curnow, who arranged the illustrations. Finally, without the interest and help of my wife, I would never have completed the work.

Hugh McKay

This paperback edition has been revised by Ken Watson of Sydney and we thank him for his contribution.

Hugh McKay and P. R. Smart
1971

The authors are grateful to the following publishers and authors for permission to reprint extracts from the books mentioned:

George Allen and Unwin Ltd, *The Hobbit* by J. R. R. Tolkien.
Angus and Robertson Ltd, *Ash Road* by Ivan Southall.
The Bodley Head, *Flood Warning* by Paul Berna.
William Collins Son and Co. Ltd, *The Once and Future King* by T. H. White.
Faber and Faber Ltd, *Salar the Salmon* by Henry Williamson.
Hamish Hamilton Ltd, *Hiroshima* by John Hersey and 'The Tiger who would be King' from *Vintage Thurber* by John Thurber, Copyright © 1963.
Hodder and Stoughton Ltd, *High in the Thin Cold Air* by Sir Edmund Hillary and D. Doig.

Michael Joseph, *The Kraken Wakes* by John Wyndham.
Kaye and Ward Ltd, *Legend of the Cid* by Robert Goldston.*
Oxford University Press, *Beowulf the Warrior* by Ian Serraillier.
Blackwood and Janet Paul Ltd, *Ice Cold River* by Ruth France.
A. H. and A. W. Reed, *Wonder Tales of Maoriland* and *Myths and Legends of Maoriland* by A. W. Reed.
Vallentine, Mitchell and Co. Ltd and Mr Otto Frank, *Diary of a Young Girl* by Anne Frank.

Our thanks to Colin McCahon, Sidney Nolan and Ross Ritchie for permission to reproduce their paintings, and to Sunday Reed, the owner of Sidney Nolan's work. Photographs supplied by the Australian News and Information Bureau (Ned Kelly); John Fairfax and Sons Ltd, Sydney (Bushfire); the New Zealand Campaign for Nuclear Disarmament; Twentieth Century-Fox Film Corporation (still from Dino de Laurentiis' film, *The Bible*); John Turner (Northland Panel); and Qantas (Sidney Nolan's *Ned Kelly*).

*From *Legend of the Cid* by Robert Goldston, first published in Great Britain by Edmund Ward (Publishers) Ltd in 1965, original edition published by the Bobbs-Merrill Co. Inc. in 1963, Copyright © 1963 by Robert Goldston, by permission of Kaye and Ward Ltd, London.

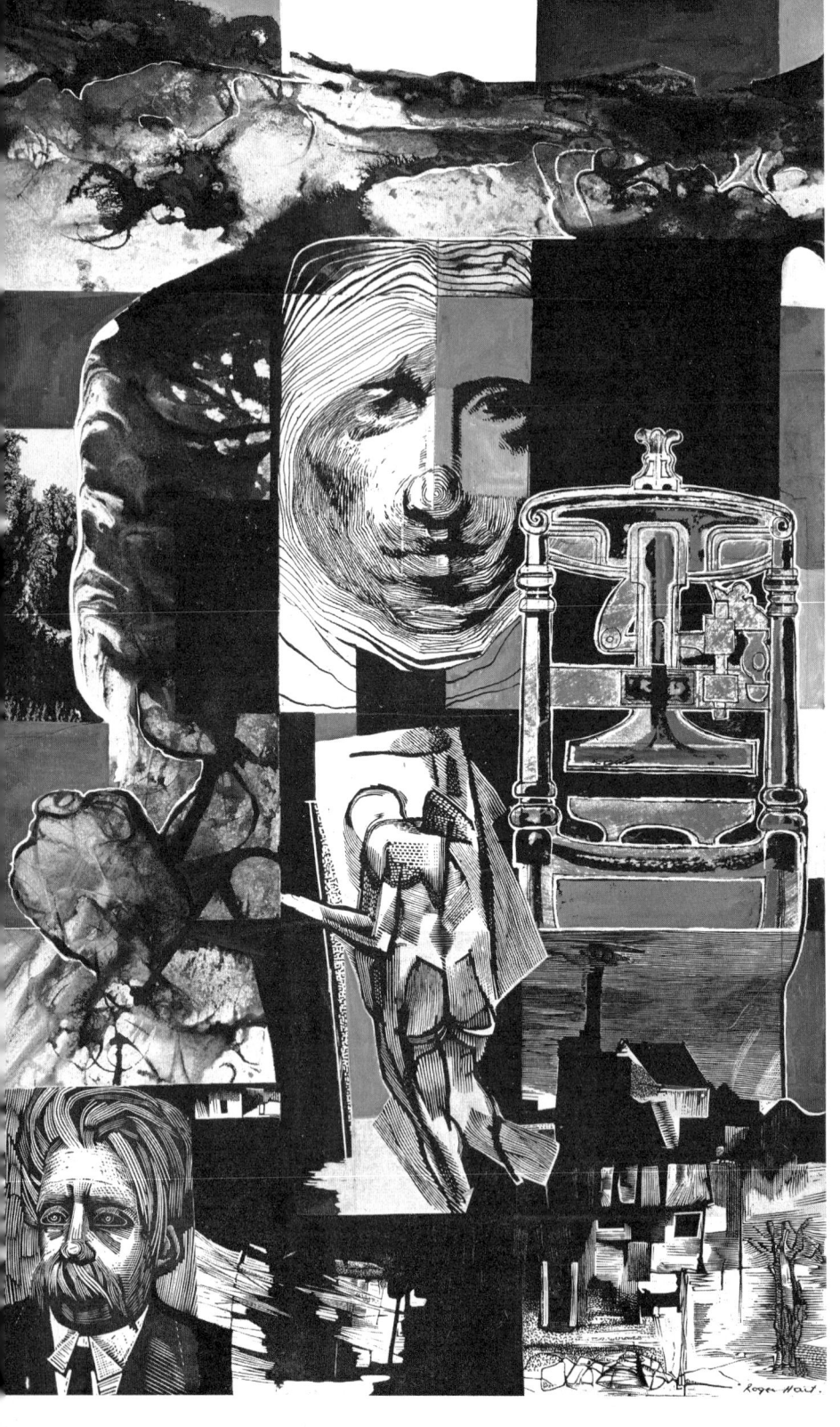

Roger Hart.

THE WORLD
OF
IMAGINATION

TOPIC 1

IMAGINATION

1. Definition
What do we mean when we say:
  i. His writing is dull. It lacks *imagination*.
 ii. It was an *imaginative* plan, no one would expect a daylight escape.
iii. Ghosts are just a figment of our *imagination*.
 iv. *Imagine* that you are walking down a deserted street of a strange town.
  v. He wrote a series of letters between two *imaginary* people.

2. Discussion questions
  i. How can physique be developed?
 ii. How are minds developed?
iii. Is imagination a separate part of our mind?
 iv. How can you tell whether you are imaginative?
  v. Has everyone the same amount of imagination?
 vi. How could you develop your ability to imagine?

3. Imagination and Work
What demands upon the imagination might the following people have to make?

i. doctor	v. carpenter
ii. manufacturer	vi. housewife
iii. saleswoman	vii. research scientist
iv. shipwrecked sailor	viii. teacher

4. Imagination and Leisure
To what extent, and in what ways, do you use your imagination in

the following leisure activities:

i. reading the newspaper	vi. tramping
ii. gardening	vii. dressmaking
iii. playing a team game	viii. stamp collecting
iv. listening to the radio	ix. caring for a pet
v. watching television	x. reading a book

5. Creativity

i. What are the distinguishing characteristics of a creative person?
ii. What is creative writing?
iii. Is there a difference between an intelligent person and a creative person?
iv. How is imagination related to creativity?
v. Why are creative people needed in our society?
vi. Why are creative people sometimes not accepted until after their deaths? Can you think of any cases of this happening?

6. Conclusions

i. How would you define *imagination*?
ii. How important is *imagination* going to be in your life?

TOPIC 2
MYTH

Question + Imagination = Myth

1. Questions

If you cannot give a satisfactory answer to each of the following questions, try to explain in each case why you cannot answer.

  i. Why does the earth spin when it moves through space?
 ii. Why is your blood red and not green?
iii. How much could be removed from your body before it ceased being you?
 iv. Why is it wrong to tell a lie, even when no one is affected by the lie?
  v. If God created man, why did he use so many different skin colourings?
 vi. What exactly did Jesus Christ look like?
vii. What kind of cars will be on our roads in the year 2000 AD?
viii. Why do some people have quick tempers, while other people never get upset?
 ix. What did you think of your father when you were three years old?
  x. Why was the word *table* chosen to represent a table? Why shouldn't it have been *taleb*, for example?

2. Myths

When mankind cannot find reasonable answers to his questions, about himself and his world, he usually imagines the answers. The best imaginings are accepted by others and so become public property, as *myths*. All the myths, legends (imaginative stories with some basis of fact), traditional behaviour (e.g. burying the dead), and taboos (e.g. not eating pork) can be described as the *mythology* of a people.

Try now to imagine how you might have answered the following questions when you were five years old and didn't want to ask adults for answers.

  i. Why is fire red?
 ii. Where does the rain come from, and why does it come?

   iii. Why does the sun go away each night?
   iv. Where is God? What does he look like?
   v. Why has the elephant got such a long nose?
This time, imagine you are living in prehistoric times. What answers might you give to the following questions?
   vi. Why does that girl look so like her dead grandmother?
   vii. Why does smoke and liquid rock come out of that mountain?
   viii. Why does a snake have no legs?
   ix. Why is there such a deep pool of water in this river?
   x. Why do young people get sick and die?

3. Conclusions
   i. Do myths have any useful purpose?
   ii. Could a myth turn out to be true? i.e. could question + imagination sometimes = fact?
   iii. Could myths be created today?
   iv. Why are there so few myths being made today? What do we have instead of a mythology?
   v. Why are myths or legends part of your school society? Are there any legends of great games and players, great geniuses, great practical jokes? If you live in a boarding school you will find more of the conventions, traditions, and taboos which are associated with a mythology. Why?

READING LIST
1. *Australian Legendary Tales* by K. Langloh Parker.
2. *Children of the Wind* by Rene Guillot.
3. *Chinese Myths and Legends* by Cyril Birch.
4. *The Complete Greek Stories of Nathaniel Hawthorne.*
5. *Encyclopedia of Myths and Legends* by H. S. Robinson and K. Wilson.
6. *Japanese Tales and Legends* by H. and W. McAlpine.
7. *Larousse Encyclopedia of Mythology.* Introduced by Robert Graves.
8. *Myths and Legends of Maoriland* by A. W. Reed.
9. *Myths of the Norsemen* by R. L. Green.
10. *Red Indian Folk and Fairy Tales* by R. Manning-Saunders.
11. *West Indian Folk Tales* by Phillip Sherlock.

TOPIC 3

LITERATURE

Question + Imagination + Language = Literature

1. Unusual Experiences

The following experiences have all been experienced by fourteen-year-olds in some part of the world, or in some period of time.

   i. Sailing around the Cape of Good Hope in a sailing ship, working on the rigging during a storm.

  ii. Dying of hunger in a mud hut.

 iii. Trying to walk again after losing both your legs in a car accident.

 iv. Being a famous and wealthy film star living in Hollywood.

  v. Hating someone so much that you planned and carried out a murder.

2. Individual Experiences

It is obvious that some people, therefore, have more unusual experiences than others. But since no two people lead exactly the same lives, everyone has some experience of living which is worth recording. Have you ever had any of these experiences:

   i. Feeling that you have seen a person before, although you know you could not have done so, or that you have been in a place before?

  ii. Feeling that you were about to die?

 iii. Liking a place so much that you felt you couldn't leave it?

 iv. Having been involved in an unusual accident?

  v. Someone having been unexpectedly generous to you?

3. Literature

Writers often work like this: they take some ordinary or extraordinary experience they have had themselves, or one they have heard about, and let their imaginations work on this experience; then they try to communicate the result in memorable language. The result is what we call literature.

4. Reading Imaginative Writings
  i. How will your reading of myths and literature be different to your reading of scientific textbooks or history books, etc.?
  ii. "This is nonsense: there are no such things as dragons." "Why couldn't he have put it more straightforwardly so I could understand it easily?"
  How useful are these comments and ones like them? What is meant by the reader *suspending judgment?*

5. This Book
This book tries to focus your attention on two particular areas in which writers commonly work:
  i. Man and his environment, or surroundings.
  ii. Man and his actions.
  The majority of the extracts are myths because it is in them that we can most clearly see imagination at work. The few extracts from more recent writings are designed to show you that the same kind of imaginings inspire writers in all periods. Most important of all, the themes chosen are ones which should stimulate your own imagination, and so help you understand the world in which you live.

6. Conclusions
  i. How can we learn to understand the world and our lives through myths and literature?
  ii. Is there a difference between experiences gained through literature and real life experiences?
  iii. What is the purpose of reading myths today?

7. Use Your Imagination
The illustration opposite is a reproduction of a painting entitled *Johnsonville March '48*, by Ross Ritchie. Use your imagination to describe what sort of face you think the man might have. His clothes should help, so discuss them as well. Your description could well be the beginnings of a character for a short story or novel.

THE AUSTRALASIAN SKETCHER

N⁰. 101.—VOL. VIII. MELBOURNE, SATURDAY, JULY 3, 1880. PRICE 6d.

NED KELLY AT BAY.
FROM A SKETCH DRAWN ON THE SPOT BY MR. T. CARRINGTON.

MAN
AND HIS
ACTIONS

HEROES

HERCULES

Scott Launcelot

JACK DONAHOE Ned Kelly

Ulysses

EL CID

Exploring the Theme

1. i. Take five different heroes from adventure-type TV programmes.
   Draw up a list of character qualities in the following form:

Name	Good Qualities	Weaknesses

   ii. Have these heroes anything in common?
   iii. Would you like to be one of these heroes and lead his life?
2. There are many other kinds of hero, e.g. Robert Falcon Scott, Sir
   Edmund Hillary, Donald Campbell, John Glenn. Make a list of
   people you would include in a book called *Twenty Heroes of the
   Twentieth Century*. In each case, give your reasons for including
   them.
3. The hero of mythology has many common features: he has a
   mysterious birth, performs amazing feats while still very young,
   brings trouble on himself by his own nature and usually finds his
   real identity only to die a heroic death. Underneath their delight in

vigorous adventures and fighting, most of the old hero legends are concerned with how a man should act in the face of danger.

   i. What has the old hero in common with the modern one?

   ii. Which do you think is the more interesting?

4. How do you account for the popularity of criminal heroes like Robin Hood, Ned Kelly, and Jesse James? What do these heroes have in common?
5. What is hero-worship? Why do people have heroes? What qualities would you look for in a hero?
6. Do you ever dream of being a hero? Why do most people do this? (Read *The Secret Life of Walter Mitty* by James Thurber.)
7. Is fear a normal emotion? Do heroes in TV Westerns, Thrillers or War films ever show fear? Are soldiers ever afraid in war? Are they cowards if they are afraid?
8. What makes a man want to risk his life breaking speed records, exploring, fighting wars, etc.?
9. Are astronauts heroes? Should man be experimented on by being sent into space? Some people create more fuss about animals being sent up in a rocket. Why?
10. Is it more difficult to be a hero in the twentieth century than it used to be? If you longed for heroic adventures, what would you choose to do?

THE LABOURS OF HERCULES

A GREEK HERO

Hercules, whom the Greeks called Heracles, was the strongest man who ever lived. He was the son of Zeus, Father of the Gods by a Greek princess. Hera, the wife of Zeus, angry that her husband had made another of his marriages with a mortal woman, sent two snakes to kill Hercules while he was still a baby. He and his twin brother Iphicles were lying asleep in a shield which served them as a cradle when the snakes crawled hissing towards them across the floor. Iphicles screamed and rolled out of the shield, but Hercules simply caught the snakes by their throats, one in each hand, and strangled them.

This is the first recorded of the many feats of strength and courage which were to make Hercules famous all over the world. As a boy he took more interest in fighting than in reading, writing or music and he was soon being described as the best archer, the best wrestler and the best boxer alive. Because Linus, his music teacher, beat him for not taking enough trouble to learn his scales, Hercules knocked his teacher dead with his lyre. Later in his life this sudden fury of Hercules was to cause him much sorrow; this time, however, when he was brought to trial for murder, Hercules told his judges that Linus had hit him first and that he had only been defending himself. He was, therefore, let off.

After several famous exploits as a young man, Hercules married a Greek princess and lived quietly with her, raising a family of three boys of whom he was extremely proud. But all this time Hera had been biding her time and awaiting the best moment for revenge. One day when Hercules and his family were exercising, she sent Lyssaa, the fury of madness, to Hercules. The hero in his madness mistook his family for an attacking enemy and slaughtered them. When his senses returned and he realised what he had done, Hercules, in despair, sought out the temple of Apollo at Delphi to ask the god how he could atone for the terrible things he had done. He was told to go to King Eurystheus, a cowardly weakling who was the favourite of Hera, and to serve him faithfully for ninety-nine months and to carry out ten tasks which he would be given.

Hera and Eurystheus considered carefully and chose the most dangerous tasks possible. Hera wanted to ensure that Hercules lost his life while Eurystheus was more afraid of the fame and popularity of Hercules. As High King of all Greece he wanted to show that Hercules could be found a coward and not the courageous and daring hero admired by the ordinary people.

The first Labour which Eurystheus set Hercules was to kill the Nemean Lion, an enormous beast with a skin proof against stone, brass or iron. It lived high up in a mountain cave and had killed everyone who had disturbed it. When Hercules found that his arrows bounced harmlessly off the lion, he took his great club of wild-olive wood which he carried everywhere with him, and hit it on the head; his club splintered into many pieces but the lion merely shook its head, yawned, and went back to its cave. The cave had two entrances, the smaller of which Hercules netted with a brass net to prevent the lion escaping. Then he went into the cave by the other entrance and caught the lion by the throat. Although it bit off the middle finger of Hercules' left hand, he managed to get its head under his right arm and squeeze it to death. Hercules skinned the lion by using one of its own claws for a knife and afterwards wore the skin. He then cut himself another wild-olive club and reported back to Eurystheus.

The Second Labour was far more dangerous; this time Hercules was ordered to kill the monstrous Hydra in the marshes of Lerna. She had a body like a huge dog's and eight snakes' heads on long necks. Hercules fired flaming arrows at the Hydra as she came out of her hole under the roots of a tree. Then he rushed forward and battered at the eight heads with his club; but as fast as he crushed them, other heads grew up in their place. Hercules, moreover, was plagued by a crab which Hera sent to bite his foot and distract his attention. Hercules was able to break the crab's shell with his foot and as he did so, he called to Iolaus, his chariot driver, to bring him a flaming torch. Drawing his sword, he cut off each head and, before it could grow, he singed the neck with the flame. That was the end of the Hydra. Hercules dipped his arrows in her poisonous blood, thus ensuring a painful death for anyone they struck.

The Third Labour of Hercules was to capture the Ceryneian Hind, a white deer with brass hooves and golden horns, belonging to the goddess Artemis. It took Hercules a whole year to catch the hind. He chased her up hill and down dale all over Greece until at last he shot an un-poisoned arrow at her as she ran past him; the arrow went through the sinew and bone of her forelegs without drawing a drop of blood and pinned them together. As she stumbled and fell, Hercules seized her, drew out the arrow and carried her on his shoulders to Eurystheus. Artemis would have been furious if he had killed her pet hind but she forgave him because she admired his clever shooting. Eurystheus immediately set the hind free in fear of angering Artemis.

Hercules' Fourth Labour was to capture the Eurymanthian Boar, a huge creature with tusks like an elephant's and an arrow-proof skin. Hercules chased it to and fro across the mountains in the winter until it stuck fast in a deep snow drift. He jumped in after it and tied its hind-legs to its forelegs. When Eurystheus saw Hercules carrying the boar on his back and striding up his palace avenue, he ran off and hid in a big brass jar.

Next Hercules was ordered to clean King Augeias's cattle yard in a single day. Augeias owned thousands of cattle and never troubled to get rid of the mess they made. Eurystheus set him this Fifth Labour just to annoy Hercules, hoping that he would cover himself with filth as he loaded the dung into baskets and carried it away. Augeias himself jeered at Hercules and bet him twenty cattle to one that he could not clean the yard in one day. Hercules accepted the bet, knocked down the yard wall, borrowed a mattock and quickly dug a couple of channels from two nearby rivers. The river water rushing through the stables cleaned them in a few minutes.

As his Sixth Labour, Eurystheus told Hercules to clear the Stymphalian Marsh of its brass-feathered, man-eating birds. They were shaped like herons but their sharp beaks could pierce even an iron breast-plate. Hercules tried to reach the birds but he was unable to walk across the marsh because the mud would not bear his weight; nor could he swim through the mud; and when he shot his arrows at the birds they glanced off the brass feathers. Fortunately for Hercules, who this time seemed defeated, the goddess Athene, admiring his courage and honesty, appeared and handed him a brass rattle. Hercules took her advice and shook the rattle. The birds rose into the air, mad with terror. He shot scores of them as they flew off towards the Black Sea for they had no brass feathers on the undersides of their bodies. None ever returned to the marsh.

The Seventh Labour given to Hercules was the capturing of a bull which had become the terror of the people of Crete. It chased farmers and soldiers, battered down huts and barns, trampled cornfields flat and frightened women and children. The bull had appeared as a sign of the kingship of King Minos but had brought suffering to the people when the King kept it instead of sacrificing it to the gods. Hercules tracked the snow-white animal, with golden horns, to a wood. There he climbed a tree and, when the bull passed underneath him, he jumped on its back. Then, after a hard struggle, he managed to clip a ring through its nose and take it safely across the sea to Eurystheus.

The Eighth Labour was to capture the four savage mares of the Thracian King, Diomedes. Diomedes fed these mares on the flesh of strangers who visited his kingdom. Hercules sailed to Thrace, landed near the palace and went straight to Diomedes' stables. He soon frightened away the grooms and began driving the mares kicking and plunging down to the sea shore. But, alarmed by the noise, Diomedes called the palace guard and hurried in pursuit. Hercules left the mares in charge of his groom, Abderus and turned to fight. The battle was a short one. Diomedes was stunned by Hercules' club and then eaten by his own horses who, unfortunately, had also devoured Abderus who could not control them. Before he left Thrace, Hercules instituted annual funeral games in honour of his groom. Then, finding his ship too small for all four mares, he harnessed them to Diomedes' chariot and drove home by way of Macedonia.

The Ninth Labour was to get a famous golden girdle from Hippolyte, Queen of the Amazons, who lived on the southern coast of the Black Sea, and bring it back as a present for Eurystheus's daughter. Hercules reached Amazonia without danger. There Queen Hippolyte fell in love with him and he could have had the girdle as a gift had not Hera interfered. Disguising herself as an Amazon, she spread a rumour that Hercules had come to kidnap Hippolyte and carry her away to Greece. The angry warrior-women rushed to rescue their Queen. In the confusion which resulted the Queen was accidentally killed by her own subjects and Hercules was forced to take the girdle from her dead body and sail away. This Labour cost Hercules dear, for he would have liked to marry Hippolyte and he hated giving the girdle to Eurystheus's daughter.

For his Tenth Labour Hercules was set to steal a herd of red cows from King Geryon who lived on an island near the Ocean Stream which surrounded the world. The main difficulty in this task was to drive the cows all the way back to Greece and both Hera and Eurystheus felt sure the time limit of ninety-nine months would run out before Hercules could accomplish his task. When Hercules reached the western end of the Mediterranean Sea where Spain and Africa were joined he cut a channel between them to save himself some time; even today the cliffs on either side of the strait are called the Pillars of Hercules. Then he sailed out into the Ocean in a golden boat lent by the Sun, using his lion-skin for a sail. As he landed on Geryon's island, a two-headed dog attacked him; he struck it dead with a swing of his club and made short work of a couple of herdsmen who came to the noise of the dog. Lastly Geryon himself rushed from his palace like a row of three men. Hera tried to distract Hercules by shining a mirror in his eyes; but the hero, although partly blinded by the flash, killed Geryon with an arrow shot sideways through all his three bodies. Hercules shot a second arrow and hit the goddess in the shoulder. She flew away screaming for Apollo and Artemis to draw the arrow out and prevent her suffering from the pain.

Hercules was now free to begin his task of herding the cows back to Greece. He first shipped the animals in his boat to the south coast of what is today France. Then he began driving them southwards along the coast. All went smoothly until he reached the Alps, where a servant of Hera's misdirected him. Instead of crossing the mountains he turned south and travelled all the way down the Italian peninsula. Angrily Hercules retraced his tracks but near Trieste the cows were stung by a vicious gadfly sent by Hera. The animals stampeded and Hercules was forced to track them some five hundred miles eastwards, to Crimea. There an ugly snake-tailed woman promised to round them up for him on the condition that he gave her three kisses. Hercules was desperate and agreed, though each kiss was very grudgingly given. He met no more extra difficulties from then on and eventually he brought the cows to Eurystheus just as the ninety-nine months ran out.

Hercules had now completed his punishment and should have been released, but on Hera's advice Eurystheus said, "You did not perform my Second Labour properly because you called on your charioteer to help kill the Hydra. And the Fifth Labour was also unsatisfactory because Augeias paid you for cleaning his cattle-yard. Therefore you must do two more tasks before I free you.

Hercules protested that Hera had interfered by sending the crab and that he had simply won a wager with Augeias; but all to no avail. The only concession that Eurystheus made was that there would be no time-limit for the two extra tasks.

The first of these Labours was to fetch the Golden Apples of the Hesperides from the Far West. These apples were the fruit of a tree once given by Mother Earth to Hera as a wedding present. The apples were guarded by the Hesperides, the daughters of the Titan Atlas, and by Ladon, an unsleeping dragon who lay coiled around the tree.

Hercules visited the Caucasus to ask the advice of Prometheus. It was then that he was able to release Prometheus from his punishment by shooting the eagle. In return he was warned not to pick the apples himself because any mortal who did would drop dead. The only thing to do was to persuade an Immortal to pick them.

Hercules went to the Titan Atlas whose punishment was to hold up the heavens on his shoulders. Atlas was willing to pick three of the apples from the tree guarded by his daughters if Hercules first killed the dragon and if Hercules held up the Heavens for an hour. Hercules shot the dragon with his bow and then took the weight of the Heavens on his head and shoulders.

Atlas soon had the apples and then suggested to Hercules that he should carry the apples to Eurystheus because he could get there so much quicker. Although Hercules knew at once that Atlas would never return, he pretended to trust him. He asked Atlas to allow him a moment in order to fold up his lion-skin to make a more comfortable pad for his head.

Atlas laid down the apples and did what Hercules had asked. Because he was so intent on fooling Hercules he was fooled himself. No sooner had the Titan taken the weight again than Hercules picked up the apples and walked away. "You were caught in your own trap," called out Hercules. After several further adventures Hercules brought the apples safely to Eurystheus.

The last Labour was the most difficult and dangerous of all. His task was to capture the dog Cerberus who guarded the gates of Hades' territory of the Underworld and to bring him back to Earth. Before descending into the terrifying depths of the Underworld, Hercules cleansed himself of all defilement at Demeter's temple. He then made the descent to the river Styx but Charon the boatman refused to ferry a live mortal across the River of Death. Hercules threatened to wreck the boat and fill its owner as full of arrows as a hedgehog has on his back. Charon gave in and ferried Hercules across, although he was later punished by Hades for his cowardice.

Persephone, the wife of Hades, pleaded on Hercules' behalf, begging her husband to allow him to take the watch-dog for a few days. Hades consented, only if Hercules mastered the dog by his own strength. If Hades thought that this was a safe condition, he was disappointed. Hercules' lion-skin was proof against the barbs of the dog's tail and he quickly gripped the animal around its neck until all three heads turned black. In this way Hercules dragged Cerberus up to earth. Eurystheus took one look at the animal and turned and hid himself until Hercules sent it back to Hades. Thus Hercules was freed from his labours and atoned fully for his crime.

Unfortunately, not long after the completion of his Twelve Labours, he had to undergo another period of servitude. Hera had been storing up her hatred since Hercules had wounded her with his arrow and now she sent another attack of the same mad anger in which Hercules again committed murder. For this crime

Hercules was sentenced to spend a year as the slave of Omphale, Queen of Lydia. To his shame he was dressed as a woman, handed a distaff, the symbol of female subjection, and set to spin wool with the other female servants of the household.

Hercules, however, was able to assist the Queen by killing a horde of brigands who were attacking passersby and also by killing a fearful monster which had begun to devour her subjects. For these deeds Omphale restored Hercules' freedom.

After this the hero was able to settle down and remarry and gain honour from peaceful feats of skill in wrestling at the Olympic Games, which he founded. He was also able to take vengeance on all those who had treated him scornfully during his Labours.

But Hercules was not destined to die a peaceful death. His wife, Deianeira, fearing that she would lose the love of Hercules, soaked one of her husband's robes in the blood of the Hydra because Hera had told her that if she did this Hercules would never be unfaithful again. No sooner had he put on the robe than he was devoured by an inner fire. Maddened with pain he tried to tear the robe off, but merely succeeded in pulling away lumps of flesh with it.

Realising that he was doomed he begged his friends to carry him to Mt Oeta and to build a funeral pyre of oak and wild olive there. They obeyed him tearfully. Hercules climbed to the platform at the top and calmly lay down on his lion-skin, using his club as a pillow. His bow and arrows he gave to the man who lit the pyre. Thus he let himself burn to death; the fire hurt far less than the maddening pain of the Hydra's poison.

Zeus felt proud of his son and at the moment of his death, there was a clap of thunder and a flash of lightning and Hercules disappeared from the eyes of men. He was admitted to Olympus where he was even reconciled with his old enemy, Hera. He married her daughter and from then on lived the blissful and magnificent life of the Immortals.

Deianeira, hearing that her jealousy had caused Hercules' death, took a sword and stabbed herself.

Discussion and Research
    a. Was Hercules just a *muscle man*?

b. What are the advantages and disadvantages of having a temper?

c. Give examples of the bad effects of panic.

d. Is it true that if a person is good at one thing, he is often good at everything?

e. Is it murder to kill an enemy in wartime?

f. The cowardly Eurystheus is typical of many of the Kings in Greek mythology. What qualities do you think rulers of countries should have?

g. Make a list of trade names which use Greek heroes (e.g. Ajax). Is there a good reason for the association?

Use Your Imagination

a. Invent ten modern labours for a modern Hercules (e.g. a Superman or Batman).

b. Dramatise the story of the Eleventh Labour of Hercules.

c. Write a story about a trickster who was himself tricked.

d. Write, *The Ballad of Hercules.*

e. Write a fairy story for your young brother or sister, e.g. Further Adventures of Jack, or Goldilocks, or Little Red Riding Hood.

f. Look at paintings of Hercules, e.g. *Hercules Slaying the Hydra* by Pollaiuolo, or *Hercules and Queen Omphale* by Gleyre. How does the artist imagine Hercules? What characteristics does he emphasise?

g. Listen to *Omphale's Spinning Wheel* by Saint-Saens. How does the composer imagine the story?

THE HOUND OF ULSTER

A CELTIC HERO

The great hero of Ulster during the years when King Connor and his Red Branch knights made Ulster the most powerful kingdom in the whole of Ireland, was a young man who died at the age of twenty-four; this was Cuchulain, the Hound of Ulster.

Connor's Red Branch knights were a body of champion warriors, chosen for their bravery and strength, and specially trained in the arts of war. The King took particular pride in this body of men who lived in the King's own hall.

Connor was determined to make Ulster strong enough to deter any enemy, and especially Queen Maeve of Connaught, from attacking it. Every summer young men from all over the kingdom came to the King's palace to be trained by the King himself and his Red Branch knights. The sons of nobles and chieftains always aspired to become members of this select group and Connor set up a training-school for these boys. As soon as each showed himself a potential knight, Connor gave him a complete war outfit: spear, sword and shield.

One summer while the King was watching his boy-troops, he noticed that one of them, a smallish boy called Setanta, excelled all the others. Connor was so pleased with the boy's performances that he called him over, praised him, and invited him to attend a great banquet that evening, at the house of Chulain, the chief blacksmith of the King.

That evening when all the guests were seated around the banquet table Chulain set on guard his watch-dog who was the most savage hound in the country, with the strength and fury of a hundred ordinary dogs. No warrior was needed on watch when Chulain's hound stood at the door. The feast had no sooner started than the animal set up a ferocious barking and at that instant the King remembered little Setanta whom he had forgotten.

The King and his followers rushed outside and in the light of the torches they saw the boy standing in front of the door with the great hound dead at his feet. As the watch-dog had sprung at him, Setanta had seized it by the throat and dashed its brains out against the pillarstone of the house. The great warriors were all the more astounded by this deed when they learnt that Setanta was just seven years old!

Only Chulain could not join in the celebration; he stood silently over the body of his faithful hound. Seeing this, Setanta called out to him:

"O Chulain, I will search all the land until I find another hound for you as good as this one you have lost. Until that time I will be your hound and guard your house and lands."

This pleased all the company greatly and they christened him Cu Chulain, or the Hound of Chulain and by that name was he known all his days.

Cuchulain's birth, like that of so many heroes, had been a

mysterious one. His father was said to be the sun-god Lugh and he had been brought up by a foster-mother until he entered the boy-troops of King Connor. He remained with the boys for almost another year after receiving his new name. Then, one day Cathbad the Druid, while he was teaching the boys, uttered a prophecy:

"The youth who takes up arms this very day will become famous all over Ireland for his heroic deeds; yet his life will be short and fleeting."

At once Cuchulain left his lessons and went straight to the King to ask him for arms. Connor gave the boy the usual equipment of a boy-warrior but Cuchulain broke the spears merely by testing them in his hands. Likewise the boy broke the weapons of a normal warrior and it was only when the King gave him weapons made for himself that Cuchulain could not break them.

To perform a deed worthy of receiving arms, Cuchulain drove off in Connor's chariot to the fort of three men who had long been the scourge of the Ulster warriors. When Cuchulain challenged them to come out and fight him, the evil brothers only laughed at the boy. Cuchulain was so angry at this treatment that he killed the eldest of the brothers with a sling shot, lopped off the head and bound it to his chariot-rim. The other brothers came out to avenge this deed only to be killed by the sword. With all three heads on his chariot rim Cuchulain returned to King Connor with a present of three of his bitterest enemies.

During the next ten years of his life Cuchulain had many great adventures and performed many heroic deeds. He was, therefore, not more than seventeen years of age when the war between Connaught and Ulster that had been expected for so long, began. The evil Queen Maeve decided to invade Ulster for the sole purpose of capturing the Brown Bull of Cooley. This was no ordinary animal for it was large enough for fifty boys to play on its broad back and it had the strength of fifty ordinary bulls. The Queen wanted this magic creature because it was the only one in Ireland that could match the White-Horned Bull of Connaught which belonged to Maeve's husband Ailell. Thus began the tragic episode that has been called ever since the Cattle Raid of Cooley.

With a huge army under her leadership, Maeve crossed the boundary into Ulster. As guide and general she had the great Ulster warrior Fergus who had been exiled by King Connor for carrying out a terrible revenge. Although Fergus hated King Connor he still loved his old comrades of the Red Branch knights and he secretly sent a message to them warning of the danger that was approaching.

Queen Maeve, however, had chosen her invasion to coincide with the period (at the beginning of winter) when all the warriors of Ulster were stricken with a sleeping sickness, the punishment for insulting a goddess many years earlier. Thus, as the Connaught army crossed into Ulster territory only the young Cuchulain, alone of the Red Branch knights, was not under the spell of the sickness. As the son of a god he was immune.

Hidden among rocks or trees, Cuchulain continually harried the advancing army. Progress was slow because of the winter snows. Every time a chariot had to be dug out of a snowdrift a number of men would be found dead. Cuchulain never rested and every night a hundred men would be slain as they slept. Maeve tried to bribe the terrible Hound of Ulster who was, single-handed, causing such havoc among her troops. Cuchulain scorned all her promises of gifts until Fergus persuaded him to stop his harrying tactics and to fight a single champion each day. Maeve's army would advance so long as the combat lasted; as soon as the Connaught champion was slain they would camp for the rest of the day. But Cuchulain slew every warrior who came before him so quickly that by the end of a week the army had scarcely advanced a single mile. In desperation Queen Maeve broke her word and sent a never-ending stream of champions to attack Cuchulain. Even then no one could stand against his strength and skill and he slew them all.

But while Cuchulain was fully occupied killing the Connaught champions, the cunning Queen sent off a raiding party to capture the Brown Bull of Cooley. When he discovered he had been tricked in this way, Cuchulain retired to his solitary camp to consider his future course of action. Immediately his father, the sun-god, put a deep sleep on him. For three whole days he slept, his wounds were healed, and he was filled with a new strength.

During those three days Maeve's army were held in check by the great courage of Connor's boy-troops. They were all too young to be affected by the sleeping sickness and three times they attacked, until after the third time they all lay dead.

At the very moment that the last boy warrior was killed, Cuchulain awoke from his sleep and his fury was terrible when

he learnt of the sacrifice of the Ulster children. Single-handed he drove into the enemy, killing with his spear, his sword and the knives on his chariot wheels until the dead were piled high on the plain. This disaster forced Maeve to hold a council of war with her leaders. So far the two greatest champions of the Connaught army, Fergus and a young man named Ferdia, had refused to fight with Cuchulain. Fergus had been a comrade in the Red Branch knights and Ferdia had been Cuchulain's best friend, the two sharing many adventures together.

Urged by Maeve's taunts of cowardice, Fergus was forced to meet Cuchulain in battle. Neither wished to fight and Fergus would not take his sword with him. Together they agreed to a mock fight which would satisfy Maeve. Cuchulain was to run from Fergus this time but if they met again it would be Fergus who would turn and flee.

When Fergus returned to Maeve the Queen could no longer reproach him but she wanted Cuchulain dead and was determined not to return to Connaught until she had been brought the hero's head. Therefore she sent for Ferdia and ordered him to fight and kill the Hound of Ulster. Neither by threats nor by bribes could the evil Queen make her greatest warrior fight his dearest friend. Finally she threatened to have her bards make up songs and poems about him which would make him known throughout Ireland for all time as the warrior afraid to fight a man. Sadly Ferdia took up his arms and climbed into his chariot. No man could face such immortality.

Cuchulain tried to persuade his friend not to fight but there was nothing that either could do. All day they fought but they were so well matched that neither could gain mastery over the other. When evening fell they stopped fighting and clasped each other in friendship. Ferdia sent half his food and water to Cuchulain and in return Cuchulain sent his friend half of his store of healing medicines. The next morning as the two champions were arming Cuchulain again tried to persuade Ferdia not to fight. The Connaught champion replied that it was the fault of no one save the Queen if either was killed.

All that day they fought savagely until each was badly wounded. Again at dusk they laid down their arms and parted in friendship. The third day's fighting was just as fierce but at the end of the day they turned away from each other without a word. Both knew that the next day would bring the death of one of them,

or of both. Near sunset of the fourth day when both were overcome by exhaustion and pain, Ferdia drove his sword so deep
into Cuchulain's body that he was unable to draw it out. With
his last ounce of strength Cuchulain threw his barbed javelin,
Gae Bolg which never failed to kill and which he had refrained
from using against Ferdia. The weapon passed clean through
Ferdia's battered shield, his breastplate and right through his
body. Cuchulain forgot his own pain and picked up his friend
carrying him in his arms to the bank of a stream. There Ferdia
died in the arms of his slayer and best friend.

After this tragic fight Cuchulain lay wounded and mourning
and refused to fight against the warriors of Connaught. It was
only the sudden awakening of King Connor and his Red Branch
knights that saved Ulster from defeat. Gathering together all his
mighty soldiers, the King soon understood the situation and fell
on the unsuspecting army of Queen Maeve who had been cele-
brating their seeming victory. The battle was one of the most
terrible ever fought, neither army being able to gain the upper
hand. Cuchulain took no part in the fighting until King Connor's
magic shield cried out for help. With his wounds still bleeding
Cuchulain joined the battle. Fergus, who hated the King, was just
about to kill him when Cuchulain appeared. Fergus was reminded
of his promise to flee and kept his word. Seeing their leader
running, apparently in defeat, the rest of the Connaught army
turned and followed him.

Although Maeve had lost the battle and the war she had
captured the Brown Bull of Cooley. Unfortunately for her, as
soon as the Brown Bull caught sight of the White Bull of Connaught they fought. The Brown Bull gored and killed the White,
raged up and down Connaught trying to find its way back to
Ulster until at length it fell dead.

For seven years after this Cattle Raid of Cooley there was
peace throughout Ulster and the Red Branch knights journeyed
far and wide over Ireland in search of adventure. But all the
time Maeve was treasuring up her hatred of Cuchulain in her
heart. She gathered around her all those who hated or envied
the great hero. When her plans were laid, she sent secretly a
force of warriors into Ulster. At the same time she had her
most powerful sorcerers put spells on Cuchulain. Despite what
everyone told him Cuchulain came to believe that Ulster was
being attacked by a huge army. He armed himself to go and

meet the enemy although many terrifying omens and signs indicated that evil and death was ahead.

He came upon Maeve's warriors by the side of a lake. Each of his three spears he threw in turn. The first was flung back at him killing his chariot driver; the second killed his horse; the third killed the great Cuchulain himself. Before life departed from his body, Cuchulain dragged himself to drink from the lake. Then he tied himself to a rock so that he might die on his feet and facing his enemies. At long last when they were sure that he was dead, a group of them came closer to the body. The leader cut off Cuchulain's head to take back to Maeve, but as he did so the sword fell from Cuchulain's grasp and sliced off the man's hand.

This was the end of the short life of Cuchulain, the Hound of Ulster, the greatest of all warriors.

Discussion
   a. What are the advantages and disadvantages of boarding-school life?
   b. How valuable in character building are organisations such as the Boy Scouts and Girl Guides?
   c. Why is the Army (Navy or Airforce) not the prestige career it once was?
   d. If you wanted to search for adventure today, where would you go and what would you do?
   e. Would you rather have a short life and fame, or a long peaceful life and be forgotten after your death? Would you make the same choice as Cuchulain?
   f. Do you think that *the pen is mightier than the sword?*

Use Your Imagination
   a. Write a dramatic dialogue, in several scenes, between Ferdia and Cuchulain.
   b. Write a ballad about Cuchulain.
   c. Describe a long fight or duel between two evenly matched opponents.

ULYSSES THE WANDERER

A GREEK EPIC HERO

In the ninth year of the Siege of Troy, one of the leaders of the Greek army, Ulysses (or Odysseus) conceived an ingenious plan to get into the city of Troy. He had his men build a huge wooden horse, hollow inside, in which twenty-four of their best soldiers were hidden. To mislead the Trojans the rest of the Greeks boarded their ships with all their equipment and sailed away leaving only the wooden horse on the seashore.

The Trojans awoke and found their enemies gone. Many of them left the city to examine the deserted shore and the huge wooden horse. While they were arguing about the significance of the horse a scruffy-looking Greek soldier was captured. He said his name was Sinon and he spun the Trojans a cunning story. The goddess Athene, he said, had commanded the Greeks to build a wooden horse in return for granting them a fresh wind home. It was vital that the horse was made too big to go through the gates of Troy, for the Trojans would be unbeatable if they had the horse within their city. Sinon himself had been chosen as the sacrificial victim but had been able to escape and hide from the Greeks until they left. He supposed that another victim had been slain in his place.

There were still some doubters, among the Trojans, who wanted the horse burnt, but Sinon's story had convinced most of the citizens. Consequently they set to work and opened a gap in the walls, large enough to allow the horse to be dragged inside.

That evening the beautiful Helen, who had been the main cause of the war, went down from her chamber to inspect the horse because she suspected a trick. She had always been admired for her skill at mimicking the voices of other people, and now she called out to all the Greek leaders in the voices of their wives. The men inside almost gave themselves away and Ulysses was forced to hold one of his homesick companions so tight that he accidentally strangled him.

Near midnight when all the city was asleep after the day's celebrations, the Greeks inside the horse opened the trap-door which had been so well concealed in the left flank of the horse and opened the gates of the city to their comrades who had sailed back under the cover of darkness.

Before its citizens were awake, the city of Troy was on fire and its King and nobles dead. Only the prince Aeneas escaped with his family and according to legend it was he who founded the city of Rome which later came to rule the world.

By their ruthless destruction of the city and its holy temples the Greeks gained the displeasure of the gods and most of them met great difficulty in returning home. The last to reach his native home was Ulysses, who did not see his wife and family until after ten years of wanderings.

Upon leaving Troy, Ulysses sailed for Thrace. There he and his men plundered the rich city of Ismarus. A priest of that city whose life he spared gave the Greeks several jars of a special wine and, before setting out on their long journey home, they drank themselves into a drunken sleep. Many of the men lying asleep on the beach were slain by a group of inland Thracians who had been attracted by the flames of the burning city. Ulysses hastily forced the remainder of his men back to their ships and the fleet put to sea at once.

They had not been rowing for long when a fierce gale began to blow the ships southwards through the Aegean Sea. They were blown past many small islands until at last the winds dropped enough to allow the fleet to put into a sheltered bay on the island of Cythera, right at the southernmost tip of Greece. A lull in the storm persuaded Ulysses to put to sea again and he set his men to row around the lee of the island and then northwest for Ithaca their home. The gods were determined not to let Ulysses off so lightly and the winds began to blow even more strongly than before. For nine days it blew and the fleet were forced ever further to the southwest towards the island of the Lotus-eaters.

The lotus was a delicious, yellow fruit much like a cherry but it had the effect of making everyone who tasted it forget completely their past lives. Ulysses sent a party ashore to the island with orders to fill the water jars. His men were offered the lotus by the friendly inhabitants and immediately lost all desire to return home. When they had not returned after several hours Ulysses led a search party to look for them. He had to drag the men back by force and chain them to the rowing benches. They wanted nothing but to spend the rest of their lives with the Lotus-eaters.

The ships set out again northwards until they reached a fertile island off the coast of Sicily. Leaving most of his men to replenish provisions by shooting some of the wild goats that inhabited the island, Ulysses set out to explore the Sicilian coastline opposite. Along the cliffs his men noticed several large caves and climbed up to see what they contained. They entered one of the caves and found to their surprise that they were inhabited, for in front was a sheep pen and inside there were some huge cheeses hanging from the wall in baskets.

Cheerfully the men killed a lamb, roasted it over a fire and enjoyed their first good meal for a long time. Unfortunately they did not know that this was the home of Polyphemus, one of the man-eating Cyclops. The Cyclops were one-eyed giants who lived as shepherds along these coasts.

That evening Polyphemus drove his sheep and goats into the cave, closed the entrance with a huge boulder, and sat down to milk his goats before he noticed Ulysses and his men. Ulysses asked the Cyclops for hospitality but, in answer, Polyphemus picked up two of the sailors, one in each hand, dashed their brains out on the side of the cave, and sat down to eat them for his supper. There was no way of escape for the terrified Greeks. Polyphemus was too big to attack and the stone at the entrance of the cave was too heavy to shift.

Next morning Polyphemus ate two more of the men and then drove his animals out of the cave, not forgetting to roll the stone over the door. Ulysses' brain worked desperately all day to find a means of escape. In the cave he found a wooden stake, the end of which he sharpened with his sword. Again Polyphemus ate two of the men when he returned but this time Ulysses offered him a bowlful of the wine his men had brought with them. The Cyclops had never tasted wine before and it pleased him greatly. He asked Ulysses what his name was, promising that he would be the last one eaten. Quickly Ulysses told the giant that his name was Nobody.

After more wine Polyphemus fell into a drunken sleep. As soon as the giant had begun to snore, Ulysses took his sharpened stake and put the point into the fire. Then he crept quietly behind the giant's head and drove the stick into his single eye. The eye sizzled and Polyphemus screamed in agony. Ulysses only just avoided the giant's hand as he lashed out in the dark. His screams soon attracted several of the other Cyclops who gathered outside his cave. They called out to Polyphemus, asking him what was disturbing him.

"Nobody", roared the giant in his pain; "Nobody has blinded me!"

On hearing this, his brothers left him alone, just as Ulysses had hoped they would.

The Greeks in the cave were able to keep out of reach of the groping hands of Polyphemus until morning came. When he realised that the sun was up, the giant opened his door enough to let one of the animals out at a time. Ulysses saw his opportunity and before all the animals had passed through he ordered his remaining companions to hold on to the underside of the animals. As each passed out of the cave, Polyphemus ran his hand over its back, but not its underside, and in this way the men escaped from their terrible prison.

Ulysses could not forbear from shouting a rude remark to the giant as the men pushed their ship into the water. This nearly proved their undoing for Polyphemus picked up a huge boulder and hurled it in the direction of the noise. If it had hit the ship it would have shattered it, but luckily it fell just to one side, making a wave that nearly turned the ship over.

Ulysses rejoined his fleet and they were nobly entertained at their next stopping point, by King Aeolus, the Guardian of the Winds. As the Greeks were making their farewells, Aeolus gave Ulysses a large leather bag which was firmly tied at the neck. In it, the King said, were all the storm winds and unless they were let out, the Greeks would have fair weather for their journey home. If a wind was needed they should let just a tiny bit out of the bag.

Under these conditions the fleet made good time across the seas to Ithaca and they were almost in sight of its shores when the men on Ulysses' ship found the opportunity they had been waiting for. They felt sure that the leather bag contained some valuable treasure which Ulysses did not mean to share with them. While Ulysses slept, the men opened the bag to see what was in it. All the storm winds escaped at once and the ships were driven right back to Aeolus again. Although Ulysses begged the King to help him a second time, Aeolus bluntly refused, telling him to use his own strength.

Their next call was at Formiae in Italy and here again they struck trouble. The fleet was beached because they were out of water and here they were caught by the inhabitants, the Laestrygones, who hurled rocks down from a cliff above the Greeks.

Ulysses escaped in a single ship, many of his men being killed and eaten by the Laestrygones.

A strong southerly gale then blew his ship to the island of Aeaea, the home of Circe, a beautiful sorceress who turned all those who visited her island into pigs. Circe fed the men Ulysses had sent to explore and at once they became pigs. Only one escaped because he had feared a trap and had not touched any of the magic food offered to him. He brought the news to his leader, who was in despair. Fortunately, Hermes answered their prayers and told Ulysses that moly, a plant with a white flower and a black root, was a charm against the magic of Circe.

Thus Ulysses was able to show Circe that her magic would not work on him, and to force her to change his men back into their normal shapes. Circe came to love Ulysses and he and his men stayed as her guests for three years. She helped Ulysses to visit the Underworld to ask advice on how to get home. There the Greek leader talked with many of his comrades who had been killed in the war and received the advice he needed.

As soon as he could, Ulysses left Circe and began his efforts to return home. Thanks to the advice he had been given he was able to avoid the next danger. His ship had to pass the island of the Sirens, who were sea maidens whose songs were so beautiful that they lured all passing ships on to the hidden reefs which surrounded their island. Ulysses put wax pellets in the ears of his men and had himself lashed to the mast so that he could enjoy the ravishing melodies of the Sirens without being able to throw himself into the sea. When he heard the music, Ulysses threatened to kill all his crew members if they did not untie him. But, as the men could hear neither the Sirens nor their leader, their ship escaped disaster and it is said that the Sirens committed suicide because their powers no longer worked.

Next Ulysses had to choose whether to take his ship the long way around the island of Sicily or to take the short cut through the strait separating Italy and Sicily. This was a most dangerous passage because on one side lived Charybdis, a sea-monster who dragged passing ships down to the depths by a fearful whirlpool; and on the other side of the strait lived Scylla, a six-headed monster who lived on the cliffs. Ulysses decided to take the risk but as he steered well clear of Charybdis he came too close to Scylla. She leaned over from her cave and snatched six of his sailors out of the boat.

The wanderers landed at Thrinacia, after passing through the strait, to wait for a favourable wind to make the crossing to Ithaca. Their provisions were low and despite Ulysses' stern warnings, his men shot some of the holy cattle of the sun, and for this they incurred the wrath of the gods.

No sooner had they set sail than Zeus hurled one of his thunderbolts at the ship, which broke into pieces and sank. Only Ulysses, who had been asleep when the cattle were killed, was not drowned. Clinging to a piece of broken mast, he drifted on the seas for nine days and was at last washed up on the shores of Calypso's island more dead than alive.

Calypso was a beautiful nymph, the daughter of Atlas, and she fell in love with Ulysses, cared for him, and treated him royally. For five years Ulysses stayed as her guest but even though she promised to make him immortal, he longed to return to his wife Penelope and to his home in Ithaca.

Athene heard his prayers and Calypso was ordered by the gods to let her prisoner go. Ulysses built a raft and left the island. He was just in sight of Scheria, the island of the Phaeacians, when his raft broke up in heavy surf, leaving him to swim ashore naked and defenceless.

Exhausted, he fell asleep on the warm sandy beach where he was discovered by Nausicaa, the daughter of the King of the island. She brought him clothes from the palace and took him to her father. After hearing Ulysses' account of his wanderings, the king gave him a ship and a crew to take him back to his homeland.

The sailors left Ulysses on his native shore more than nineteen years after he had left for the Trojan War. At that time his son Telemachus had been merely a babe in arms; now he was a strong young man who spent his time searching for his lost father. Ulysses' wife, the beautiful Penelope, had been plagued for several years by a hundred suitors who encamped in her palace waiting for her to choose one of their number to be her husband. She continued faithful to her husband and had never given up hope that he might yet return to her. Therefore, she had kept postponing the moment she must choose one of the suitors. By now, however, they were becoming more and more impatient and she had been forced to promise them that she would make her choice as soon as she had finished a garment she was weaving. She worked all day at her loom but secretly at night she went and unpicked all she had done during the day.

The suitors were planning to kill the young Telemachus and if Ulysses had suddenly turned up at his palace they would have killed him straight away. Athene chose to help Ulysses again and she disguised him as an old beggar. In this disguise he learnt what was happening at his palace from one of his old servants called Eumaeus. When Telemachus returned from one of his trips in search of information about his father, Eumaeus met him before he fell into the clutches of the suitors and brought him to his father. Between them they devised a plan for getting rid of the suitors and of restoring Ulysses to his rightful place.

Telemachus went secretly to his mother and persuaded her to announce to the suitors that the next day she would choose as husband the one who could shoot best with a great bow that had belonged to Ulysses, and one that only he could use. The suitors celebrated well that night and when they had fallen into their drunken sleep, Telemachus removed all their weapons from the hall.

At the test the next day all the suitors failed even to string the bow which had not been used since Ulysses' departure. Ulysses himself, in his beggarly disguise, had come to watch the proceedings and finally among insults and laughter was allowed to try his skill with the bow. He strung the bow easily enough and before the suitors knew what was happening he began shooting them one by one. Eumaeus shut the door of the hall and Ulysses was joined by Telemachus and his sword. Together they killed the rest of the suitors.

Ulysses had little time to settle down and reorganise his kingdom before the relatives of the dead suitors came in force to demand revenge. Ulysses and his followers began another slaughter but this time the gods interposed and brought peace. Thus Ulysses and Penelope were able to live peacefully for the rest of their lives.

Discussion

    a. What qualities of personality did Ulysses have?

    b. What is the connection between *Sirens* and sirens?

    c. Do you think the marriage service is reasonable in asking a husband and wife to be faithful, "until death do us part"?

    d. Was Ulysses courageous to risk passing between Scylla and Charybdis or was he thoughtless in risking the lives of his men? How responsible should a leader be for the safety of his men?

Use Your Imagination

a. Invent two more adventures for Ulysses before he gets home.
b. Write a play about Ulysses' homecoming.
c. Write the lyrics for the song the sirens sang.
d. Write the diary of a Lotus eater.
e. Write on *Absence makes the Heart Grow Fonder*
    or: *The Pleasures of Coming Home.*
f. Write The Ballad of Ulysses and the Cyclops.
g. Look at paintings of Ulysses, e.g. *Polyphemus Derided by Ulysses* by Turner, or *The Return of Ulysses* by Pintoricchio. What aspects of the story is the artist emphasing?
h. Listen to *Sirens*, Part 3 of *Nocturnes* by Debussy, as a great composer's imaginings of the song of the Sirens.

SIR LAUNCELOT OF THE LAKE

A BRITISH HERO

King Arthur was crowned King of Britain at the age of fifteen and his early years were spent in defeating both the Saxon invaders and the rebel lords who had refused to accept him as king. During those early years Arthur drew around him a faithful group of warriors. But when peace was restored to the troubled country, Arthur's greatest problem was to prevent this group of warriors from fighting among themselves. For this reason King Arthur instituted the Round Table and the knightly order of chivalry which it symbolised. In this way Arthur tried to channel the strength and vigour of his warriors into a positive attempt to establish order and justice throughout the land.

The Round Table itself was in Arthur's castle at his capital of Camelot. Only knights who had proved their valour and who had sworn to uphold goodness and virtue, to fight evil and wickedness, to give help to all those who asked for it, and never to harm a woman, could gain a place at the table. It became the ambition of all heroic young men to prove themselves worthy of this honour. The greatest of the knights of the Round Table were men like Sir Gawaine, Sir Tristram, Sir Geraint, Sir Gareth, Sir Percival, Sir Bors, Sir Galahad and the most famous of them all, Sir Launcelot of the Lake.

Sir Launcelot was the son of King Ban of Brittany but while he was still only a baby in his mother's arms he was taken away from his family by the fairy Lady of the Lake, who educated the boy and taught him the arts needed by a knight. This is why Launcelot was known all his life as Sir Launcelot of the Lake.

On his eighteenth birthday Launcelot was sent to King Arthur's court by his foster-mother. There, however, he was laughed at by many of the knights for physically he was a very tall man with the clumsy awkwardness of such men. But even at such a youthful age, Launcelot was more than a match for many of Arthur's well-tried knights. The laughter turned quickly to admiration and occasionally to jealousy when he demonstrated his ability with the lance and the sword.

Launcelot had not been at court for very long when an old and feeble woman, with white hair and a gentle face, was shown into the audience room. The King silenced the conversation and noise of his knights and asked the woman what she wanted.

"Justice, Lord Arthur", was her reply. Then she told them her tale. She and her son had built a tiny cottage on a little patch of land that they had cut out of the marshlands not far to the south of Camelot. Although the marshes were dominated by the cruel Sir Caradoc of the Dolorous Tower, the two were sure that their little patch of land would be too small and humble to attract the knight's attention. They had been drawing a meagre existence there for several years when suddenly Sir Caradoc sent soldiers to tear down their tiny cottage and to send them out of his lands. The old woman's son went to plead his case with Sir Caradoc but was whipped and thrown half-dead at his mother's feet as she waited outside his castle. The woman had tended her son's injuries and then sought out Arthur's court to beg for justice.

The King asked his knights if any of them knew this unworthy knight.

"Yes, Sire," one replied; "his castle is just on the edge of the marshes and anyone who tries to pass through his lands he tortures and kills unless they pay tribute money to him. He is a brother of Sir Turquine who fought against us during the wars."

Arthur was very angry to learn of such injustice so close to the

very heart of his kingdom and he called for one of the knights
to bring the cruel and evil Sir Caradoc to Camelot to stand trial.

Not one of the knights was prepared to carry out this mission
for they were fearful not only of Sir Caradoc but also of Sir
Turquine, who had the reputation of being the strongest warrior
in the whole country.

The King was greatly ashamed of his knights and he had just
called for his own armour when young Launcelot asked permission to carry out the task. The King would not hear of
sending the young untried man but Launcelot was persistent and
his determination so impressed the King that he said:

"Very well, you shall be my messenger. Tell Sir Caradoc that
King Arthur demands his presence to answer the complaints of
this old woman. If he refuses to come, or if he harms my messenger
in any way, I will come and take his life and burn his castle to
the ground."

The enemies that Launcelot's skill with lance and sword had
made were pleased to get rid of the youth, for they were sure
that Sir Caradoc would slay him. But two days later young
Launcelot came back to Camelot and with him, tied securely on
the back of a horse, was a red-faced knight who continued all
the time to swear and curse against Launcelot.

"Here, my Lord, is Sir Caradoc of the Dolorous Tower in the
Marsh," said Launcelot. "He would not come when I gave him
your message and so I waited until he had gone to bed drunk
with wine. Secretly I carried him out of the castle and tied him
on the horse as you see. Now, my Lord Arthur, if you would
give me knighthood, Sir Caradoc could be tested by me in the
tilt-yard."

The King tried to persuade Launcelot to let an older man take
his place in the test of Sir Caradoc. Neither would Launcelot
desist nor could the King find anyone to take his place. Sir
Caradoc continued to pour scorn on the *milky boy* and no sooner
had the King knighted Launcelot than the two were on their
horses charging at each other. Sir Launcelot for one of the few
times in his life was knocked from his horse by his opponent.
Quickly he was on his feet with drawn sword. By rule of knightly
combat, Sir Caradoc should have dismounted and fought hand-
to-hand, but instead he turned and rode straight at Sir Launcelot
with the intention of pinning him to the ground with his lance.
The young man avoided Sir Caradoc's first charge with a nimble

side-step and stood waiting for the second. Sir Caradoc wheeled his charger but the shouts of the other knights at his cowardly actions forced him to throw down his lance and attack his opponent with his sword.

Sir Launcelot, despite his youth, was a master swordsman and, defending himself from the ferocity of Sir Caradoc's attack, he bided his time until he saw his opportunity. With his first attacking stroke he split the knight's helmet and his strength was such that the traitorous knight was beaten to his knees.

Sir Launcelot called upon him to yield and confess his guilt but he would not. Then the young man struck him between the neck and head and slew him.

Thus ended Launcelot's first great deed at the court of King Arthur. Launcelot was given Sir Caradoc's castle and land and his very first action was to give the old woman and her son a fair piece of land and a cottage. All the wrongs which had been done by Sir Caradoc were righted and a new era of peace and happiness came to the people of the Marshes.

Soon after this King Arthur married the beautiful Gwenevere and their marriage was celebrated by a knightly tournament in which Sir Launcelot proved himself the champion of all the Knights of the Round Table. In honour of the Queen many of the knights set out from Camelot in search of adventure.

Sir Launcelot set out with his cousin, Sir Lionel, and the two rode northwards for two days until they came into an open forest. The forest made Launcelot feel very sleepy and he lay down under a tree to sleep while Sir Lionel sat down on guard. Sir Lionel was just beginning to feel drowsy in the warm summer weather when he heard the clink of armour and three knights riding their hardest galloped past him, followed by a single huge knight in hot pursuit. The single knight overtook each of the knights in turn and smote them to the ground. Then he returned, dismounted, and flung each of the stunned knights on his horse and tied them there with the reins, before riding off, driving the other horses ahead of him.

Sir Lionel was just going to awaken his cousin when he thought that here was an opportunity to gain a victory of his own. He sprang on his horse and called a challenge to the great knight. Not many moments later Sir Lionel was trussed up on the back of his horse like the other three.

While Sir Launcelot still lay asleep under the tree, he was

seen by four beautiful ladies on white mules who passed by the same way. Unfortunately one of the ladies was the evil Lady of the Marshes, the sister of Sir Caradoc; the others were the witch queens who were continually struggling against King Arthur's attempts to bring goodness and peace to his realm. They recognised young Sir Launcelot immediately and put an enchantment on him. When at length he awoke, he found himself not in the forest but in a bleak and narrow dungeon cell. All night long he racked his brain to work out what had happened to him. He heard nothing; no one came near him.

Finally the next morning a servant girl in rags brought him a piece of dried bread and a little water. From her he learnt the cause of his imprisonment and he began to despair. But the servant girl said that she would help him escape on one condition. Quickly she told him her story. She was the daughter of a noble knight who had been captured by a strong and cruel man, Sir Turquine, who owned a castle nearby. She had been given to Sir Turquine's sister, the Lady of the Marsh, to work as a kitchen maid. The girl's daring plan was to steal the keys of the castle and show Sir Launcelot the way out; her condition was that he make an attempt to rescue her father from Sir Turquine's castle.

Sir Launcelot did not take long to make up his mind. He knew that Sir Turquine was the brother of Sir Caradoc and he knew also that Sir Turquine had publicly proclaimed that he would kill all King Arthur's knights and in particular Sir Launcelot, in revenge for his brother's death.

The girl left him, promising to return with the keys late at night. Sir Launcelot waited as the hours passed slowly. Then in the middle of the night his rescuer brought the keys to unlock his cell door. Soon the two of them were in the stable where Sir Launcelot found his armour and his horse. Quietly they unlocked all the doors that led to their escape. Sir Launcelot galloped into the forest as soon as they were out of the castle. He left the girl in the care of a convent of nuns and the next morning followed the way she had told him to the castle of the tyrant knight.

Fixed on a prominent tree outside this castle, Sir Launcelot discovered the shields of many knights of the Round Table including that of his cousin Sir Lionel. The mighty knight who had so easily defeated Sir Lionel was none other than Sir Turquine himself.

Sir Launcelot called out a challenge and as soon as Sir Turquine knew it was a knight of the Round Table he rode out to accept the challenge. So began the hardest fight that Sir Launcelot ever had in his long life. The two knights missed each other on the first charge and on the second the impact of their blows was so great that the backs of both horses were broken and both knights flung on the ground. Both lay stunned for a long time. Then they set to with sword and shield, hacking at each other for nearly two hours, with neither knight gaining mastery over his opponent.

Resting for a moment on his sword, Sir Turquine then said to Sir Launcelot, "You are the best swordsman I have ever met. I will set free all of King Arthur's men and we will become friends as long as you are not that Sir Launcelot of the Lake who slew my brother, Sir Caradoc."

Sir Launcelot revealed his name to the other and declared that he had slain Sir Caradoc in fair combat.

Then replied Sir Turquine, "You are the most welcome guest I could have at my castle. Come, we will never part until one of us is dead."

And they ran at each other in fury until both were covered with the blood of the other and the ground upon which they were fighting was slippery with their blood. In the end the strength of the younger man began to tell and Sir Turquine's shield began to drop lower and lower in his weary arm. Launcelot was heartened by this sign and attacked with a renewed vigour. Soon the mighty Sir Turquine lay dead on the ground.

Sir Launcelot washed his wounds in the river and as soon as he had recovered a little he went into the castle and released all the prisoners including Sir Lionel his cousin, and the father of the girl who had helped him escape. Not even pausing to hear the grateful thanks of those he had rescued, he rode off into the depths of the forest to rest and recover from his wounds.

Many were the adventures he had after this mighty victory and many were the people he rescued from one predicament or another. At last the time of the year when all the knights of the Round Table met at Camelot to renew their vows came around and Sir Launcelot turned back towards King Arthur's court. As he was riding through a pleasantly wooded countryside, he came upon a lady who stood weeping beneath a great oak tree. The lady begged him to climb the tree and recapture her husband's hawk which had slipped her grasp. She pleaded that her husband had such a savage temper that he would kill her if she returned without his hawk.

Launcelot did as his vows required although his skill at climbing trees was not as great as his skill in jousting or sword-play. He had to remove his armour to climb into the trees and he soon had reached the cord the hawk was tied to and dropped it down to the woman. He was just about to clamber down again when a knight came out of a hiding-place with a drawn sword in his hand. Sir Launcelot had been caught in one of the traps set by the Lady of the Marsh who now had two brothers to revenge. It was also one of the most awkward situations Sir Launcelot ever found himself in. Totally defenceless, he had neither weapon nor armour to protect himself. Desperately he broke off a dead branch, and leaped on to the ground. He rolled over and warded off a savage sword stroke as he sprang to his feet. Then he swung his make-shift club and cracked his enemy a blow on the head. With his own sword he cut off the man's head with a single stroke, put on his armour, and rode off leaving the woman bewailing the death of her husband.

He rode on towards Camelot and paused to rest for the night at a castle of a friendly knight. There he was able to rescue Sir Kay, one of Arthur's first knights, who was being pursued by three hostile knights. Sir Kay thanked Sir Launcelot graciously when he recognised him. He was a rather unfortunate man who was a very poor jouster and made up for this by a very caustic tongue. This had naturally won him many enemies who used to delight in knocking him off his horse whenever they met him. Sir Kay confessed his fears of riding into Camelot the next day and when he awoke the next morning he found Sir Launcelot already gone and with him Sir Kay's armour. Sir Kay, therefore, put on the armour of Sir Launcelot and rode completely unchallenged into Camelot. But Sir Launcelot, wearing the armour of Sir Kay, was challenged about a dozen times and left about a dozen knights on their backs before riding into the town.

The next day all the knights were gathered around the Round Table and when they heard the trick that had been played on them there was a great deal of laughter and joking. Sir Kay then told the King how Sir Launcelot had rescued him from the three knights. All the knights who had been held prisoner by Sir Turquine told of their rescue and the great fight between the strongest knights in the world. The stream continued; almost all the knights were able to recount some noble deed of Sir Launcelot and all who were present were left in no doubt as to who the best and strongest of King Arthur's knights was.

Many other adventures of Sir Launcelot are told in the chronicles. You can read of his strange madness and how he spent many years as a mad hermit; you can read of his guilty love for Arthur's queen, Gwenevere, which brought an end to the Round Table and you can read of his search for the Holy Grail and of his disappointment in not being chosen as one of the three holiest knights in the world; and finally you can read of his part in the death of King Arthur, his great sorrow, and his peaceful end.

Discussion

a. King Arthur tried to *channel strength and vigour*. How is this done today?
b. Is the chivalrous knight's attitude to women out of date?
c. What are the qualities of a gentleman?
d. How satisfactory do you think was the practice of *testing* a man's guilt, by making him fight in single combat? How do we *test* a man today? Does this have any disadvantages?
e. Discuss the idea that jealousy is a horrible disease.

Use Your Imagination

a. Write a story about Sir Launcelot from an enemy's point of view.
b. Write a story about someone who has a physical deformity and suffers because of it. Your character may turn the tables at the end of the story.

MAUI AND THE SUN GOD

A MAORI MYTH

In the days when Maui lived with his brothers, everyone grumbled because the days were so short. Each morning the sun bounced out of the sea and travelled quickly across the sky. It was very awkward, but although everyone grumbled about it, no one did anything until Maui came along. Only Maui watched the sun hurrying across the sky. Only Maui thought and thought until at last he knew what he had to do.

"Don't you think the days are too short?" he asked his brothers.

"Yes," they said. "They are not long enough for us to hunt, or fish, or work in our kumera gardens. That is why we have to play our games in the dark."

"Then we must make them longer."

They laughed at him. "You are always trying to do the impossible, Maui," they said. "Is the sun a bird, to be caught while it perches on a branch?"

"Yes," Maui replied. "I will catch it as if it were a bird sitting in a tree."

The brothers laughed louder still. "You must think you are a god, if you want to catch the sun."

Maui was growing angry. "You forget too quickly," he said. "You forget that it was Maui who tamed the fire you use. I am stronger than men, but I need your help. Tomorrow we will get up early and travel to where the sun rises. We will make a net of strong ropes and catch him, and tame him as if he were a bird."

He looked at them so fiercely that they were frightened.

"We would help you," they told him, "but it would be no use. The ropes would burn. The sun is so strong and fiery that the thickest ropes would burn, and we would be shrivelled up in the heat."

"Get your wives to bring flax and we will make the ropes now, before it gets too dark," Maui ordered. They called their wives and told them to bring the green flax leaves. Maui sat down with them and showed them how to plait them into strong ropes. Some were flat, others were round and some were square, when they were finished. These were all the ways of plaiting flax which the Maori people still remember, though it was long, long ago when Maui first taught them how to make them. By the time night came they had a great pile of rope.

"Now we can sleep," Maui said, as then sun rushed from the sky and the twinkling stars came out all over the beautiful blue cloak of Rangi, the Sky Father. "We shall set out very early in the morning."

And so they did, long before the sun poked his head out of the sea, and the sky was still very grey and cold. All that day they travelled, carrying long coils of the flax ropes. All the next day they kept on walking, and the next, until they reached the hiding place of the sun. In the daytime they hid, but at night they came out and built a strong high wall of clay right on the edge of the world. When the sun rose they would be able to shelter behind it

from the heat. At the ends of the wall they built houses made of branches of trees. Above the place where the sun would rise they set a big noose and covered it with branches and green leaves so that it could not be seen.

When everything was already they hid in the houses at the end of the wall, Maui in one and his brothers in the other. Presently the light grew stronger and stronger until they could hardly bear to look at it. Then a shaft of sunlight rushed across the wall. The brothers had one end of the flax rope in their hands.

"Steady," whispered Maui. "Wait till his head and paws are through the noose. A-ah! Now!"

The brothers pulled at the rope as hard as they could. Maui held the other end. The noose fell over the head of Tama, the sun. Maui and his brothers felt him plunge and struggle like a fish caught by a hook.

"Hold tight," Maui called. They set their feet against the wall and tugged and tugged.

Tama, the sun, saw the wall, and the huts made of branches, and the ropes that stretched to the doors of the huts. He was angry and roared with pain. He caught the rope in his hands and tried to break it, but it was too strong for him. He pushed with his feet against the earth, till the rope sang like insects in the bush in summer-time, and it began to slip through the fingers of the men who were holding it.

Then Maui tied the flax to the door of his hut and rushed out, bending low so that he was hidden by the wall. The fiery rays of the sun scorched his back and burnt his hair, but he rose up, shielding his face with his arm, and struck the sun with a heavy club. It was a magic weapon, made from one of the bones of his old grandmother.

Again and again he struck the sun god, until he stopped struggling and cried with pain. He fell on his knees and said, "Stop! Stop! Do you want to kill me?"

"No," Maui replied. "I am sorry I had to hurt you, Tama, but it was the only way to make you go more slowly. When you leap across the sky, the day goes so quickly, that down on earth there is not time for us to do all that we want. If I let you go now, will you promise to go more slowly, so that the days will be longer?"

"Yes," said Tama. "Your magic weapon has taken all my strength from me. I could not go quickly, even if I tried."

"Let go the ropes," Maui ordered his brothers. When they fell away, Tama stood up and began his journey across the sky. He went slowly, slowly, slowly, as he does to this very day.

Discussion

a. Is it a waste of time trying to *do the impossible*?
b. What things that were once thought impossible, are now regarded as commonplace?
c. What things do you grumble about most? Can you do anything about them?
d. Maui *watched* and *thought*. Does this make him a scientist? How does a scientist work?
e. There are two contrasting elements in stories: the *romantic*, or that which is impossible and fantastic; and the *realistic*, or that which is real and everyday. What things in the story of Maui would you call romantic? What realistic?

Use Your Imagination

a. Write a story about somebody who tries to do something which is impossible.
b. Write a story about a time when you found the day too short to do all the things you wanted to.
c. Prepare and perform the story of Maui and the Sun as a mime.

EL CID'S LAST VICTORIES

A MEDIEVAL SPANISH HERO

(Rodrigo de Vivar, or El Cid, the Lord Conqueror, received his title when his bravery and military skill were able to unite Christian Spain against the Moslem Moors who had controlled Spain for three hundred years. Towards the end of his life El Cid was determined to provoke the Almoravide Emperor, Yusuf, to send his armies in support of the Moors and thus remove any further threat by defeating them. Accordingly, he laid a trap by besieging the last Moorish fortress of Murviedo.)

Within two weeks The Cid had prepared a small army of five thousand men. He led them from his capital Valencia at night and spread rumours that they were off on a raid into Granada. They followed the road to Granada that led past the great city-fortress of Murviedo, and early one morning not long after, its mighty walls and towers came into view. The Almoravides within the city, seeing that The Cid led such a small army, believed the rumours and assumed he would never dare attack Murviedo. They simply closed their gates and waited for the Christians to pass by. But to their surprise they saw Rodrigo's men encircle the city and pitch their tents as if for a long siege. They were confident that The Cid could never storm the walls of Murviedo. But they had neglected to gather food and provisions for a siege. And they could not believe that The Cid did not have some huge army lurking nearby. In their confusion they sent off messengers to Yusuf seeking advice and aid. The Cid's men could easily have captured these messengers, but they had orders to let them get away.

Now The Cid sent for siege engines. These were giant catapults that could throw great boulders against the walls, towers on wheels in which soldiers could hide while they were rolled up against the battlements, huge battering rams and so forth. His small army presented every appearance of being determined to besiege Murviedo indefinitely.

When Emperor Yusuf in Africa received news of The Cid's intentions, he pondered the matter deeply. He could not afford to lose the fortress of Murviedo. But he could not believe that The Cid seriously thought of storming the place with a mere five thousand men. Then it must all be a trap! Perhaps King Alfonso, The Cid's overlord, was waiting with a huge army nearby. Perhaps the infidels expected Yusuf to rush to the defence of Murviedo and thus be caught between the jaws of two armies at once. Yusuf smiled. He was not so easily fooled. If the unbelievers had set a trap for him he would spring it on them! Calling his advisers, he ordered the assembly of a huge army. "The infidel dogs think to trap me before the walls of Murviedo," he announced. "But I will attack them where they least expect it. I will lead this army personally to seize Valencia itself. The Cid expects me to fight for Murviedo and so I shall—by seizing his own stronghold! Between Valencia and Murviedo I will crush this insolent Cid as one would crack a nut between two stones! We sail within a fortnight!"

Thus it was that the Emperor Yusuf led a mighty army—the flower of all his forces—in a sudden attack on Valencia itself. His fleet crossed the sparkling waters of the Mediterranean swiftly and landed his army on a sandy beach not ten miles from The Cid's capital. Then, to the sound of the dreaded Almoravide drums, this mighty host marched upon the city. Within a few days it was under siege. With The Cid gone, and his best knights with him, Yusuf expected Valencia to fall within a matter of days.

But Yusuf had walked right into the trap after all. For Rodrigo and his counsellors had guessed exactly what the Almoravide emperor would do. They had known he would suspect the attack on Murviedo to be a trap, and putting themselves in Yusuf's place, had seen that an immediate attack on Valencia would be his best plan. They had prepared accordingly.

Inside this supposedly defenceless city, twenty thousand knights, heavily armed and under the expert leadership of Alvar Háñez, stood ready and waiting to receive the Almoravide blow. Meanwhile, The Cid, kept informed by spies of Yusuf's every movement, waited until the Almoravides were firmly established before Valencia. Then, moving rapidly by night, he led his army from Murviedo and hurried back to the capital, bringing the siege engines with them.

Yusuf, unaware of The Cid's movements, ordered his army to attack at once. Wave after wave of screaming fanatics threw themselves against the mighty walls of Valencia. Alvar Háñez within the city, had ordered his men to repel these attacks, but to pretend a certain weakness. By nightfall of the first day of the siege, Yusuf was confident that the city would be his within a week.

But that very night The Cid and his men secretly camped on the hills behind Yusuf's army. There Rodrigo ordered the catapults to be set up and aimed directly down into Yusuf's camp. Then, when dawn came and the roaring Almoravide drums sent Yusuf's army once again into the attack against the city walls, The Cid ordered the catapults to open fire.

Never before had siege engines been used in warfare on the open field. It was the first use of artillery. When the great boulders crashed down among the tents and reserves of the Almoravide army, they thought the sky itself was raining destruction upon them. Their confusion and fear were increased by superstition. Yusuf now ordered back his advance divisions from the walls of Valencia to organise an attack upon The Cid's siege engines in his rear. But at that moment, The Cid, leading his five thousand knights, charged down on the disorganised Moslems. And at this signal the great gates of Valencia swung wide to disgorge Alvar Háñez and his twenty thousand horsemen onto the plain.

Trapped between two powerful forces, their lines broken by the fury of the Christian charge, the Almoravide army began to disintegrate. When they heard the dread news that The Cid himself was upon them, their terror knew no bounds. This was the terrible wizard who had drowned one of their armies. Now he caused boulders to rain on them from the sky! To fight against him was to fight against the Devil himself! Panic swept through Yusuf's army and it quickly fled desperately from the field, seeking cover from the terrible swords of the Christian knights and the even more terrible boulders from the heavens.

The Cid's victory was tremendous. Of all that vast army of Moslems no more than a handful ever returned to Africa. All the rest were either killed or captured.

But although The Cid's army suffered few casualties, the cost was great to them. For as The Cid himself was attacking Yusuf, his horse, Babieca, stumbled over a tent rope. In falling, The Cid had broken his shoulder, and he was carried unconscious back to Valencia.

Despite all possible care The Cid's broken shoulder became infected and to the grief of all Christians the Champion died. The only one to rejoice at the news was Yusuf who had been gathering together an army to repel the expected Christian invasion. Seizing the opportunity the Almoravides were soon laying siege to the city of Valencia.

Under the leadership of Alvar Háñez and Doña Jimena, El Cid's wife, the Christians turned back every attack from Yusuf. The Emperor soon learned his lesson and decided simply to starve the city into subjection. With provisions sufficient for only six months Doña Jimena appealed to Alphonso of Castile to come to their relief.

With soldiers from all over Spain a huge army was raised to come to help Valencia, Yusuf confidently planned a movement that suggested he was retreating and indeed all thought that the siege was broken. King Alfonso entered the city in triumph with all his troops.

But in the morning the Christian leaders realised that they walked into a trap. For Yusuf's men had returned to the siege during the night and moreover, they had been strengthened by the arrival of another sixty thousand Moslem warriors. Valencia was surrounded by over one hundred thousand men, the greatest army Yusuf had ever put into the field. He was determined to destroy the whole of the Christian army.

The council of the Christian leaders inside Valencia was a gloomy one. There was not enough food left to feed the army for even a week and to fight their way out of the city seemed like suicide and would only leave the citizens to be slaughtered by Yusuf. Then Doña Jimena remembered a vision that El Cid had had before his death and she outlined a desperate plan.

The following morning, at the first light of dawn, the Almoravide sentries saw the great gates of Valencia swing open. Instantly they sounded the alarm. Drums rolled throughout the huge Almoravide camp. Horses were mounted, weapons unsheathed. The enormous mass of Moslem warriors waited to throw themselves on the escaping Christians. Their spirits were high—this would be a massacre rather than a battle. Emperor Yusuf hastily mounted his horse. "Now," he muttered, "I shall slay them all. They will not pass beyond the first rank of my army. On this field Christian Spain will be destroyed beyond all hope of recovery!" He stared intently at the opened gates of the city, waiting to give the command that would hurl his army like a tidal wave upon the emerging Christians.

But suddenly a huge wail of terror went up from the advance ranks of the Almoravides. Mounted knights were emerging from the gates of the city. In their hands they bore the banners of The Cid. And at their head—no—it could not be! Yusuf cried out in surprise and dread. There was no doubt about it. It was The Cid himself who led the charge, mounted upon Babieca, his sword Tizone gleaming by his side! This was too much for Yusuf and too much for his army. The legends were all true! This Cid was really a demon from hell! Here he was, raised from the dead, charging relentlessly down upon them!

With wails of fear and screams of terror that rent the air for miles around, Yusuf's army fled. They did not even attempt to fight and neither did their emperor. Each of them thought only of escaping from the terrible apparition that thundered down upon them. They were certain now that the entire field was cursed and enchanted. A mighty wave of superstitious dread broke their ranks and sent them scurrying in their thousands in every direction so long as it led away from Valencia.

King Alfonso did not pursue the Almoravides. He recalled his knights who led back Babieca and the embalmed body of The Cid, which had been strapped into the saddle of his faithful horse. Thus, Rodrigo, El Cid Campeador, won his last victory after his death.

Discussion

a. What is a *psychological advantage*? Why is it important in war or in sport? How can you gain a psychological advantage over your opponents?

b. What is propaganda? What part does it play in modern war?

c. The Almoravides were filled with *superstitious dread*. Why are people superstitious? What are common everyday superstitions in our lives? Can you explain their origins e.g. throwing salt over your shoulder?

Use Your Imagination

a. Write a short story based on a person who laughs at a common superstition.

b. Write an account of El Cid's last fight from the point of view of an Almoravide captain.

BOLD JACK DONAHOE

In Dublin town I was brought up, in that city of great fame—
My decent friends and parents, they will tell to you the same.
It was for the sake of five hundred pounds I was sent across the main,
For seven long years in New South Wales to wear a convict's chain.

Chorus

Then come, my hearties, we'll roam the mountains high!
Together we will plunder, together we will die!
We'll wander over mountains and we'll gallop over plains—
For we scorn to live in slavery, bound down in iron chains.

I'd scarce been there twelve months or more upon the Australian shore,
When I took to the highway, as I'd oft-times done before.
There was me and Jacky Underwood, and Webber and Webster, too.
These were the true associates of bold Jack Donahoe.

Now Donahoe was taken, all for a notorious crime,
And sentenced to be hanged upon the gallows-tree so high.
But when they came to Sydney gaol he left them in a stew,
And when they came to call the roll they missed bold Donahoe.

As Donahoe made his escape, to the bush he went straightway,
The people they were all afraid to travel night or day—
For every week in the newspapers there was published something
    new
Concerning this dauntless hero, the bold Jack Donahoe!

As Donahoe was cruising, one summer's afternoon,
Little was his notion his death was near so soon,
When a sergeant of the horse police discharged his car-a-bine,
And called aloud to Donahoe to fight or to resign.

"Resign to you—you cowardly dogs! a thing I ne'er will do,
For I'll fight this night with all my might," cried bold
    Jack Donahoe.
"I'd rather roam these hills and dales, like wolf or kangaroo,
Than work one hour for Government!" cried bold Jack Donahoe.
He fought six rounds with the horse police until the fatal ball,
Which pierced his heart and made him start, caused Donahoe to fall,
And as he closed his mournful eyes, he bade this world Adieu,
Saying, "Convicts all, both large and small, say prayers for
    Donahoe!"
                Chorus
Then come, my hearties, we'll roam the mountains high!
Together we will plunder, together we will die!
We'll wander over mountains and we'll gallop over plains—
For we scorn to live in slavery, bound down in iron chains.

STRINGYBARK CREEK

A sergeant and three constables rode out from Mansfield town
At the end of last October for to hunt the Kellys down.
They started for the Wombat Hills, and found it quite a lark
To be camped upon the borders of a creek called Stringybark.

When Scanlon and the sergeant rode away to search the scrub,
Leaving MacIntyre and Lonigan in camp to cook the grub,
Ned Kelly and his comrades came to take a nearer look,
For being short of flour they wished to interview the cook.

Both troopers at the camp alone they were well pleased to see,
Watching while the billy boiled to make their pints of tea.
They smoked and chatted gaily, never thinking of alarms,
Till they heard the dreaded cry behind: "Bail up! Lay down
    your arms!"

It was later in the afternoon, the sergeant and his mate
Came riding blithely through the bush to meet their cruel fate.
"The Kellys have the drop on you," the prisoners cried aloud,
But the troopers took it as a joke and sat their horses proud.

Then trooper Scanlon made a move his rifle to unsling,
But to his heart a bullet sped, and death was in its sting.
Then Kennedy leapt off his mount and ran for cover near,
And fought most gamely to the last for all his life held dear.

The sergeant's horse raced through the camp escaping friend
    and foe,
And MacIntyre, his life at stake, sprang to the saddle-bow.
He galloped far into the night, a haunted, harassed man,
Then planted in a wombat-hole till morning light began.

At dawn of day he hastened out, and made for Mansfield town
To break the news that made men vow to shoot the killers down.
So from that hour the Kelly gang was hunted far and wide
Like outlaw dingoes of the hills until the day they died.

Discussion and Research

a. Find out all you can about the careers of Bold Jack Donahoe,
   Ned Kelly and other famous Australian bushrangers. Why
   do people make criminals such as these into heroes?
b. There are several versions of the ballad *Bold Jack Donahoe*.
   Can you explain why this is so?
c. Read or listen to recordings of some other ballads written
   about Jack Donahoe, Ben Hall and Ned Kelly. Read some
   modern poems about bushrangers, such as Kenneth Slessor's

THE TRIAL

Judge Barry then passed sentence of death and concluded with the usual formula "May the Lord have mercy on your soul." Ned Kelly: "Yes, I will meet you there!"

(No. 25 in the Ned Kelly series (1946–47) by Sidney Nolan)

A Bushranger and John Manifold's two poems, *Binda Ball* and *What Bill Lewis Told His Grandson*.

d. What causes people to commit crimes or to become delinquent? (You will find some suggestions in the ballads written about the bushrangers.)

e. Examine Sidney Nolan's paintings of Ned Kelly. What are your reactions to them?

Use Your Imagination

a. Design a poster offering a reward for the capture of Jack Donahoe or Ned Kelly.

b. "Come all you wild colonials and listen to my tale; A story of bushranging days I will to you unveil."
Write your own poem beginning with these lines.

c. Write a newspaper report of the death of Jack Donahoe or of the shootings at Stringybark Creek.

d. Using a tape-recorder, write and produce a short programme about the life of a famous bushranger.

e. Solitary Confinement—write about how you would feel in this situation.

SCOTT

AN ANTARCTIC EXPLORER

Letter to Sir J. M. Barrie

My Dear Barrie. We are pegging out in a very comfortless spot. Hoping this letter may be found and sent to you, I write a word of farewell . . . Good-bye. I am not at all afraid of the end, but sad to miss many a humble pleasure which I had planned for the future on our long marches. I may not have proved a great explorer, but we have done the greatest march ever made and come very near to great success. Good-bye, my dear friend,

Yours ever,
R. Scott.

We are in a desperate state, feet frozen, etc. No fuel and a long way from food, but it would do your heart good to be in our tent,

to hear our songs and the cheery conversation as to what we will do when we get to Hut Point.

Later. We are very near the end, but have not and will not lose our good cheer. We have four days of storm in our tent and no-where's food or fuel. We did intend to finish ourselves when things proved like this, but we have decided to die naturally in the track.

What lots and lots I could tell you of this journey. How much better has it been than lounging in too great comfort at home.

From Scott's, "Message to the Public"

For four days we have been unable to leave the tent—the gale howling about us. We are weak, writing is difficult, but for my own sake I do not regret this journey, which has shown that Englishmen can endure hardships, help one another, and meet death with as great a fortitude as ever in the past. We took risks, we knew we took them; things have come out against us, and therefore we have no cause for complaint, but bow to the will of Providence, determined still to do our best to the last. But if we have been willing to give our lives to this enterprise, which is for the honour of our country, I appeal to our countrymen to see that those who depend on us are properly cared for.

Had we lived, I should have had a tale to tell of the hardihood, endurance, and courage of my companions which would have stirred the heart of every Englishman. These rough notes and our dead bodies must tell the tale, but surely a great rich country like ours will see that those who are dependent on us are properly provided for.

R. Scott.

Discussion

    a. What is wrong with staying at home in comfort?

    b. Would you rather watch something or take part in it? Explain your views by referring to particular activities.

    c. Are Englishmen better at enduring hardships than any other nationality?

    d. Some people think that those who risk their lives in mountains, or on the sea, and so on, are selfish. What do you think?

    e. What did Scott achieve except the death of himself and his friends? Should he expect the state to look after his dependants?

f. Were the men commendable in their decision to die naturally rather than to *finish* themselves?

Use Your Imagination

a. Write an eyewitness account of the finding of Scott's tent.
b. Describe a modern day misadventure in Antarctica.
c. Write a poem about an Antarctic scene.
d. Listen to *Sinfonia Antarctica* by Vaughan Williams, where the composer imagines the Antarctic and man's struggle against it.
e. Collect a series of photographs or reproduction of paintings depicting the Antarctic scene. Decide which show more imagination.
f. Look at *South*, an illustrated book of Antarctica by Graham Billing (text) and Guy Mannering (photography).

FEAR

FROM *THE RED BADGE OF COURAGE*

(The youth is fighting in the American Civil War and has just withstood his first taste of real action, a charge by the enemy.)

The youth awakened slowly. He came gradually back to a position from which he could regard himself. For moments he had been scrutinising his person in a dazed way as if he had never before seen himself. Then he picked up his cap from the ground. He wriggled in his jacket to make a more comfortable fit, and kneeling relaced his shoe. He thoughtfully mopped his reeking features.

So it was all over at last! The supreme trial had been passed. The red, formidable difficulties of war had been vanquished.

He went into an ecstasy of self-satisfaction. He had the most delightful sensations of his life. Standing as if apart from himself, he viewed that last scene. He perceived that the man who had fought thus was magnificent.

He felt that he was a fine fellow. He saw himself even with those ideals which he had considered as far beyond him. He smiled in deep gratification.

Upon his fellows he beamed tenderness and good will. "Gee! ain't it hot, hey?" he said affably to a man who was polishing his streaming face with his coat sleeves.

"You bet!" said the other, grinning sociably. "I never seen sech dumb hotness." He sprawled out luxuriously on the ground. "Gee, yes! An' I hope we don't have no more fightin' till a week from Monday."

There were some handshakings and deep speeches with men whose features were familiar, but with whom the youth now felt the bonds of tied hearts. He helped a cursing comrade to bind up a wound of the shin.

But, of a sudden, cries of amazement broke out along the ranks of the new regiment. "Here they come again! Here they come ag'in!" The man who had sprawled upon the ground started up and said, "Gosh!"

The youth turned quick eyes upon the field. He discerned forms begin to swell in masses out of a distant wood. He again saw the tilted flag speeding forward.

The shells, which had ceased to trouble the regiment for a time, came swirling again, and exploded in the grass or among the leaves of the trees. They looked to be strange war flowers bursting into fierce bloom.

The men groaned. The lustre faded from their eyes. Their smudged countenances now expressed a profound dejection. They moved their stiffened bodies slowly, and watched in sullen mood the frantic approach of the enemy. The slaves toiling in the temple of this god began to feel rebellion at his hard tasks.

They fretted and complained each to each. "Oh, say, this is too much of a good thing! Why can't somebody send us supports?"

"We ain't never goin' to stand this second banging. I didn't come here to fight the hull damn' rebel army."

There was one who raised a doleful cry. "I wish Bill Smithers had trod on my hand, insteader me treddin' on his'n." The sore joints of the regiment creaked as it painfully floundered into position to repulse.

The youth stared. Surely, he thought, this impossible thing was not about to happen. He waited as if he expected the enemy to suddenly stop, apologise and retire bowing. It was all a mistake.

But the firing began somewhere on the regimental line and ripped along in both directions. The level sheets of flame developed great clouds of smoke that tumbled and tossed in the mild wind near the ground for a moment, and then rolled through the ranks as through a gate. The clouds were tinged an earthlike yellow in the sunrays and in the shadow were a sorry blue. The flag was sometimes eaten and lost in this mass of vapour, but more often projected, sun-touched, resplendent.

Into the youth's eyes there came a look that one can see in the orbs of a jaded horse. His neck was quivering with nervous weakness and the muscles of his arms felt numb and bloodless. His hands, too, seemed large and awkward as if he was wearing invisible mittens. And there was a great uncertainty about his knee joints.

The words that comrades had uttered previous to the firing began to recur to him. "Oh, say, this is too much of a good thing! What do they take us for—Why don't they send supports? I didn't come here to fight the hull rebel damned army."

He began to exaggerate the endurance, the skill, and the valour of those who were coming. Himself reeling from exhaustion, he was astonished beyond measure at such persistency. They must be machines of steel. It was very gloomy struggling against such affairs, wound up perhaps to fight until sundown.

He slowly lifted his rifle and catching a glimpse of the thick-spread field he blazed at a cantering cluster. He stopped then and began to peer as best he could through the smoke. He caught changing views of the ground covered with men who were all running like pursued imps, and yelling.

To the youth it was an onslaught of redoubtable dragons. He became like the man who lost his legs at the approach of the red and green monster. He waited in a sort of horrified, listening attitude. He seemed to shut his eyes and wait to be gobbled.

A man near him who up to this time had been working feverishly at his rifle suddenly stopped and ran with howls. A lad whose face had borne an expression of exalted courage, the majesty of he who dares give his life, was at an instant, smitten abject. He blanched like one who has come to the edge of a cliff at midnight and is suddenly made aware. There was a revelation. He, too, threw down his gun and fled. There was no shame his in face. He ran like a rabbit.

Others began to scamper away through the smoke. The youth turned his head, shaken from his trance by this movement as if the regiment was leaving him behind. He saw the few fleeting forms. He yelled then with fright and swung about. For a moment, in the great clamour, he was like a proverbial chicken. He lost the direction of safety. Destruction threatened him from all points. Directly he began to speed towards the rear in great leaps. His rifle and cap were gone. His unbuttoned coat bulged in the wind, the flap of his cartridge box bobbed wildly, and his canteen, by its slender cord, swung out behind. On his face was all the horror of those things which he imagined.

The lieutenant sprang forward bawling. The youth saw his features wrathfully red, and saw him make a dab with his sword. His one thought of the incident was that the lieutenant was a peculiar creature to feel interested in such matters upon this occasion.

He ran like a blind man. Two or three times he fell down. Once he knocked his shoulder so heavily against a tree that he went headlong.

Since he had turned his back upon the fight his fears had been wondrously magnified. Death about to thrust him between the shoulder-blades was far more dreadful than death about to smite him between the eyes. When he thought of it later, he conceived the impression that it is better to view the appalling than to be merely within hearing. The noises of the battle were like stones; he believed himself liable to be crushed.

As he ran on he mingled with others. He dimly saw men on his right and on his left, and he heard footsteps behind him. He thought that all the regiment was fleeing, pursued by these ominous crashes.

In his flight the sound of these following footsteps gave him his one meagre relief. He felt vaguely that death must make a first choice of the men who were nearest; the initial morsels for the dragons would be then those who were following him. So he displayed the zeal of an insane sprinter in his purpose to keep them in the rear. There was a race.

As he, leading, went across a little field, he found himself in a region of shells. They hurtled over his head with long wild screams. As he listened he imagined them to have rows of cruel teeth that grinned at him. Once one lit before him and the vivid lightning of the explosion effectively barred the way in his chosen direction. He grovelled on the ground and then springing up went careering off through some bushes.

Discussion

   a. Was *the youth* a coward? Will he always be a coward or was this just an accidental weakness?

   b. Discuss the way *the youth* used his imagination.

   c. Are there any times in war when a soldier should refuse to obey an order? (Read *The Big Decision* by C. S. Forester.)

Use Your Imagination

   a. What experience would frighten you the most? Describe it.

   b. Write a story showing how someone overcomes his or her fear.

   c. Write a story entitled *The Big Decision*.

Heroines

Hinemoa

AMY JOHNSON

Joan of Arc

WAR DIARY

Judith

Exploring the Theme

1. How many heroines can you think of in ordinary TV programmes? Do they have any qualities in common?
2. Compare the heroines with the heroes.
3. Why are there fewer heroines? Are women less heroic than men?
4. The Russians have sent a woman into space. Do you think this is right? Why haven't the Americans done the same?

HINEMOA

A MAORI HEROINE

On the island of Mokoia, set like a jewel on the shining surface of Lake Rotorua, Tutanekai lived with his mother and step-father and his half-brothers. Cut off from the people of the main-land, they lived their placid life untroubled by the tribal wars that raged among the people of the lakeshore. But they were not entirely isolated. Now and again the canoes that visited the mainland brought back news of the outer world. It was in such a way as this that Tutanekai and his brothers came to hear of Hinemoa, the beautiful high-born girl of Owhata. All who spoke of her told of her gentleness and beauty and strength of character. These reports so stirred the brothers that they fell in love with her before ever they saw her. The brothers of Tutanekai each boasted that he would take her to wife, but Tutanekai himself said nothing. He went out on the balcony of his hillside whare at night and looked across the dark water towards Owhata. Then he would sigh, and after a while he would bring out his flute and breathe a love-song into it.

The music carried clearly across the water and Hinemoa, sitting in the moonlight with her friends, would fall silent. The steam by the lakeside drifted above the undergrowth, restless and lost, like the thoughts of Hinemoa. She had heard of the brothers of Mokoia, and she would smile to herself and say, "That is the music of Tutanekai."

One day there was a great meeting of the tribes on the mainland. Hinemoa was there with her people, and her eyes sought out Tutanekai. Some instinct seemed to tell her that the tall, handsome young man was the flute-player of the moonlight nights. As for Tutanekai, he had not seen many young girls, but of all the lovely young women of Rotorua who were gathered together in the house of meeting, it was only Hinemoa who attracted him. In this way they became lovers, yet neither Hinemoa nor Tutanekai declared their love. The young woman of Owhata was high-born, of the line of chiefs, a puhi, and although he loved her, Tutanekai feared to risk a refusal. Yet at every gathering he sought her and spoke to her in friendly fashion. Finally he decided to send a message to her. It was taken by a friend. When this friend had told of Tutanekai's love, Hinemoa said simply, "Eh-hu! Have we then loved alike?"

The next time the tribes gathered together, the lovers met outside the meeting-house. No one missed them for the whare was full. While the laughter and cries of the dancers were loud in their ears, they sat outside in the darkness, and Tutanekai told Hinemoa his words of love. "How shall we meet?" he asked. Hinemoa's voice replied softly, "I will come to you, Tutanekai, my beloved. I must go when no one suspects, and you must be ready for me. How shall I know when you will be waiting?"

Tutanekai thought for a moment. "Already the music has

carried my love to you across the waters of Rotorua. Now let it bear another message—the message that I am waiting for you. When you hear the music in the silence of the night, you will know that I am looking for your canoe to steal across the shadowed lake."

The next night Hinemoa heard the distant flute, and stole down to the shore of the lake where the canoes were kept. They were all there, but alas, someone had beached them and they were high up on the sand. Not a single canoe was floating in the water. She could hear the music clearly across the water where the island of Mokoia lay sleeping on the quiet lake.

"Hinemoa! Hinemoa!" called the flute. "Hinemoa!" and her heart was heavy in her because of her longing for her lover. She turned away. Her people must have seen the manner of Tutanekai's glance in the meeting-house. Perhaps someone had heard them whispering together in the darkness, for it was unusual for all the canoes to be beached at the same time.

The following night she went to the lakeside, but still the canoes were high and dry, and her suspicion turned to certainty.

Every night Tutanekai's music called to her. The moon waxed and waned while love for him stirred in her so that she could not sleep, and the distant flute seemed to thunder in her ears. With her eyes closely shut, she could see Tutanekai on the balcony of his house blowing into the long putara and then putting it down and straining his eyes to see if he could catch sight of the darker shape of a canoe amongst the shadows.

Then came the moonless nights and she could wait no longer. The rows of canoes had mocked her every night and she did not even glance towards them. She had prepared six large gourds, tying them together with flax so that they would support her in the water.

As she went towards the little beach, Tutanekai's music sounded again and quickened her resolve. She threw off her single garment, a cloak of finely woven flax, tied the gourds under her armpits and waded out until she found herself being lifted by the waves. She struck out boldly. She felt like a bird which has escaped from a cage.

Presently the lapping of the waves seemed to drown the sound of the flute. Perhaps a current of air had carried the sound away from her, but she felt a moment of panic. The darkness pressed down on her like a solid wall. She tried to lift herself up to see if the island was close at hand but the darkness closed in on her. She had lost her sense of direction. She could not tell where Mokoia lay, nor the beach she had left. Her arms were tired and the gourds seemed to have lost their buoyancy, so that the little waves struck cruelly against her face and the water was cold.

She gave a cry of despair as something brushed against her face. Then with a sob of relief she caught hold of it and rested against it. It was a tree trunk floating in the water. As she held closely to it and raised herself a little above the waves, the wind brought the sound of the flute back to her ears. She pushed away from the log and began to swim steadily towards the music. The gloom had lightened and she could see the bulk of the island against the faint starlight. Sometimes she grew tired and rested, but her panic was over. Once the current carried her away from the island, but she swam more strongly and felt the water surging under her. The time passed slowly and the water grew colder. Then the music stopped and the only sound was the ceaseless lapping of the waves against her breast. She stopped and listened. At first she could hear nothing. Then a tiny sound—a crash and a hiss like a wave falling on the sand and running up the slope of the beach. Another hiss as it drained away, carrying a myriad grains of sand with it. A moment later she felt the ground under her feet.

She stumbled up the beach, half frozen. The cold wind numbed her flesh even more than the lake water. Feeling her way with her hands in front of her, she came upon some rocks. They were warm, and she could smell the sulphur-laden steam of a hot pool. Once before she had been on the island and she knew where she was. This was the hot pool of Waikimihia, directly below Tutanekai's whare.

She lowered herself gratefully into the water and felt the warmth soaking into her chilled body.

Now that she had reached her lover's home and the dangers of the journey were behind her, she felt suddenly shy and reluctant to appear before him. Her clothes lay far away on the beach at Owhata. Then came the sound of footsteps descending the path toward Waikimihia. In a flash she pulled herself towards the bank and crouched under an overhanging rock.

The footsteps stopped, something dropped into the pool, and she heard the water gurgling into a calabash close by her side. Disguising her voice, she said in a deep voice, "Where are you taking the water? Who are you?"

The man who was fetching the water started at the voice coming from the darkness.

"I am the slave of Tutanekai. I am taking the water to him."
Hinemoa's heart leaped. "Give me the calabash," she said, still
pretending to be a man. She spoke so confidently that the slave
handed the calabash to her without protest. She put it to her lips
and drank. Then, raising her arm, she hurled the empty vessel
across the pool so that it smashed against the rocks on the further
side.

The slave cried out, half in fear and half in anger, "Why have
you done that? That was Tutanekai's calabash."

Hinemoa made no reply, but only drew back further into the
shadow of the rock. The slave looked carefully over the stones but
could see nothing. "Who are you? "he called shrilly, and when
there was no reply, he turned and ran up to the whare.

"What is the matter?" Tutanekai exclaimed as he saw the slave's
face. "What has happened? Where is the water I told you to bring?"

"The calabash is broken."

"Who broke it?"

"The man in the pool."

Tutanekai looked at him closely. "Can you not speak more
clearly? Who broke it?"

"The man in the pool," the slave repeated doggedly.

For a moment Tutanekai thought of going down to find out for
himself, but he changed his mind. Night after night he had played
his flute, but Hinemoa had forgotten. He turned his face to the
wall and said wearily, "Oh, take another calabash and fetch the
water."

The slave departed on his errand a second time. He looked
round cautiously but there was no sign of any stranger, yet no
sooner had he dipped the calabash in the pool than the deep voice
called out, "If the water is for Tutanekai, give it to me."

The slave's legs trembled, but he held out the calabash at arm's
length. A hand came out of the shadows, and again the calabash
crashed against the rocks and broke.

This time the man did not wait to protest. He ran up the winding
path as swiftly as his legs would carry him.

"The second calabash has been broken by the man at the pool,"
he gasped.

Tutanekai shut his eyes. "Take another calabash," he said in a
flat voice.

In a little while the slave stood before him empty-handed once
more. At last Tutanekai felt the anger rising swiftly in him. He

forgot his longing for Hinemoa. With one swift movement he sprang to his feet, caught up his mere and ran to the pool.

Hinemoa heard him coming and knew it was her lover. The slave's footsteps had been heavy and slow; Tutanekai was running lightly and swiftly. She crouched still further under the rocks and held her breath as the footsteps stopped on the brink of the pool. The moon was rising and she saw his shadow lying across the water. Under the rocks the darkness lay heavily.

"Where are you, breaker of pots?" called Tutanekai. "Come out so that I can see you. Show yourself like a man instead of hiding like a koura, a crayfish in the water."

There was no reply. Peering through her hair, Hinemoa saw the shadow moving across the water, coming closer and closer. A hand reached down and touched her hair. "Ah!" cried Tutanekai, "I have found you. Come out, you rascal." His grip tightened. "Let me see your face."

Hinemoa stood up. Climbing slowly on to the bank, she faced her lover, beautiful and shy like the silver heron which is seen but once in a hundred years. "I am Hinemoa," she whispered.

The harshness fled from Tutanekai's face like summer clouds before the sun.

"Hinemoa!"

The smoke from the cooking fires rose straight up in the morning air as the people ate their breakfast.

"Where is Tutanekai?" someone asked.

There was no reply until his slave stepped forward. "I have not seen him since he went down to the stranger at the pool in the night," he said.

"What stranger?" they asked, and he told them of the breaking of the calabashes, and how Tutanekai went down himself to meet the stranger.

"This is strange to my ears," one of the old men said. "Perhaps something has happened to Tutanekai? He is a bold fighter, but in the night even the bravest may be worsted when the shadows conceal the thrust of a hidden weapon. Hurry to his whare and see if all is well with him."

Their eyes followed the slave as he hastened to the home of Tutanekai. In the stillness the sound of the sliding door striking the frame came like a thunder-clap.

He peered into the gloom and then went back to the people waiting on the marae. "There are four feet there," he cried. "I looked for Tutanekai and I saw four feet instead of two."

A murmur of voices came from the men and women. "Who is with him?" the old man called, raising his voice so that he could be heard.

The slave did not answer but ran back again to look. He returned shouting with excitement, "It is Hinemoa!"

His cry was taken up by the people. "Hinemoa is here with Tutanekai!"

Now Tutanekai's brothers were jealous for they had each thought that Hinemoa would choose him for her husband. "It cannot be Hinemoa," they shouted angrily. "There is no canoe on the beach, so she could not have come during the night. The slave is lying."

Then Tutanekai came out of the whare, leading Hinemoa by the hand. She held herself proudly, wearing a cloak of her husband's, and walking by his side. A great cry of welcome went up from the people, drowning the brothers' angry exclamations. "It is indeed Hinemoa. Welcome to Hinemoa!"

That is the love story of Hinemoa and her daring journey across the lake to her lover, which will be told so long as the Arawa people live by the steaming waters of Rotorua.

Discussion

a. What qualities would you look for in a wife, or husband?
b. Do you believe in love at first sight?
c. Literature is full of famous lovers. Find out about three great love affairs e.g. Tristan and Isolde; Romeo and Juliet etc.
c. What makes people shy? Is there anything a shy person can do to overcome shyness? What forms can shyness take?
e. What is there about Hinemoa that makes her a heroine?

Use Your Imagination

a. Write a poem about being frightened in the dark.
b. Prepare a modern dance version of the Hinemoa story.
c. Write about a *Journey at Night*.
d. Describe two people in love.

JUDITH

A JEWISH HEROINE

King Nebuchadnezzar of Babylon began his long reign as a weak king, so weak that the rulers of all the small nations to the west of Babylon poured scorn on his plans to overcome the mighty Persian Empire. When he asked them to send him troops to fight the Persians, they merely laughed at him and refused to give him any support.

The King, however, made careful preparations and with the skill of his greatest general, Holofernes, he won a great victory against the Persians. Their army was utterly crushed and Nebuchadnezzar became ruler of the greatest Empire the world had ever known.

One of the first things Nebuchadnezzar determined to do was to take his revenge on all those small western nations which had refused to help him. He assembled a huge army of 120,000 foot soldiers and 12,000 charioteers, and gave command of it to Holofernes, with the express order to destroy any country which refused to acknowledge his supreme power and send tribute to him.

No nation could stand against the army and soon it had assembled tremendous wealth from the nations who sought to make peace with King Nebuchadnezzar. Only one small country refused to accept the King's demands and that was the hill country of Judea. These people were Jews who had just returned from captivity and slavery and they had no army and few soldiers. As soon as they learned what had happened to their neighbours, they dispatched all their peoples to the tops of the hills which were more easily fortified. The only entrance to Judea was through a narrow pass and, to the city at the head of the pass, Bethulia, they sent all their strongest young men. Throughout the country the people stored up food and water in their cities and waited for the army of the enemy to arrive.

When Holofernes received news from his scouts that the people of Judea had fortified the tops of the hills and blocked the passes, he was very angry and called together his advisers to find out what sort of people these were who stood against him. One of his chiefs of staff called Achior told Holofernes the history of the Jews and how their God had helped them escape from Egypt by parting the waters of the Red Sea, and how more recently they had been led into captivity because they had not listened to their God. He advised Holofernes to leave the Jews well alone in case their God struck his army. For these words Achior was dismissed from his position and left in the wilderness to die. He managed to free himself and sought refuge among the people of Judea who welcomed him.

After this Holofernes was even more determined to teach the Jews a lesson and he moved his whole army into the valley that led to the pass guarded by the citizens of Bethulia. He realised at once that the city was in such an impregnable position that to capture it by storm would cost him dearly in foot soldiers. Instead he decided to cut off the city's water supply, a spring at the bottom of the hill, and simply camp there until the people died of thirst or surrendered to him.

After thirty days the people of Bethulia had used almost every drop of water to be had and a majority of the citizens were in favour of surrendering to Holofernes. But their leaders were able to make them wait another five days to see if God would help them. If, after that time, no miracle had happened, they would open the city to the Assyrian army.

One of the inhabitants of Bethulia still had faith that they would be saved. This was a beautiful young widow whose name was Judith. She was not only wealthy and beautiful but also very pious. She went to the leaders and told them that they should not demand of God in such a way. Then she asked them to let her and a maid servant out of the city gates that evening, promising that they would be free of their enemies within the five days.

She returned to her home and prayed fervently to God before dressing herself in her most beautiful clothes. Then she passed through the city gates and down the hill towards the camp of the Assyrians. The sentries were astonished by her beauty and asked her what she wanted.

She replied, "I am from the city of Bethulia. I wish to be taken to your general to show him a way to capture the city and the rest of the country."

The men wondered greatly but escorted her to the tent of Holofernes. When she was shown into his presence, she threw herself at his feet and remained there until he commanded a servant to lift her up.

"Do not fear," said Holofernes. "I will hurt no one who is

prepared to serve Nebuchadnezzar, King of the whole World. If your people had not been so stubborn I would not have been sent against them."

Judith then told him that she had heard so many good things spoken about him that she knew he was to become their ruler. She could look into the future and she had come to lead him into their capital, Jerusalem. Her country needed strong rule and he was to be their saviour.

Her words greatly pleased Holofernes who was very much taken by her beauty. For three days she stayed in the Assyrian camp, each night going out through the sentries to pray to her God. On the third night Holofernes ordered a feast and asked Judith to attend it. During the celebrations he drank so much wine that he fell asleep. One by one his other guests became weary and went to their beds, leaving Judith alone with the sleeping Holofernes.

Judith prayed to God to strengthen her arm and then she picked up Holofernes' sword and with two blows cut off his head. She pushed the body under the canopy of the bed and put the head in her bag. Then she called her maid servant and the two of them went out of the camp past the sentries, just as she had done on the previous nights.

This time, however, she returned quickly to the gates of Bethulia and asked the guards to open the gates. The leaders of the city heard her voice and came out to meet her. She called on them to praise God and then showed them the contents of her bag.

The feat of the woman astounded everyone and as one, they praised her and the work God had done through her.

The head was placed on the highest part of the wall and swiftly the Jews made preparations for the morning. Soon everyone in the city knew what Judith had done and when the sun came up every able-bodied man was waiting fully-armed outside the gates of the city.

The Assyrians thought that an attack was about to begin and they sent immediately to the tent of Holofernes to ask for instructions. Their army was already drawn up in readiness for the battle but when Holofernes their great general was found dead on the floor the word spread to all the soldiers. The shock was intense and many began to think that they were up against supernatural powers. Then one man began to run, and, before their captains could stop them, the whole Assyrian army had fled out of the valley in utter panic.

The soldiers of Bethulia and others who had heard the news fell on the retreating Assyrians and slew thousands of them and chased the rest far to the eastwards. All the spoil in the Assyrian camp was taken by the Jews and used to build their country.

Judith became the heroine of her people and gifts and blessings were poured upon her. She spent the rest of her days in Bethulia, a greatly honoured citizen, never marrying despite the many who were attracted by her beauty and courage.

Discussion and Research

There have been many infamous assassinations. Choose any three and find out about them. Report on the motives of the assassin and the consequences of the assassination.

Use Your Imagination

a. Achior's story.
b. Poem by Judith, either before or after the assassination, or both.
c. Diary of a person in the hilltop town.
d. Treachery.

JOAN OF ARC

A MEDIEVAL HEROINE-SAINT

Joan was born in the little village of Domrémy in France in the year 1410. Her father was a farmer and the headman of the village.

At that time her country, France, was split into two parts, under the two ruling families the Orléanists and the Burgundians, each of whom were struggling for supremacy. In addition, the country was being devastated by invading English armies as the King of England also claimed the French throne.

When Joan was about twelve, the wars took a new turn. Charles VI, the King of France, died. His son the Dauphin claimed the throne and rallied the Orléanists and a small army to his cause. But the Burgundians put their weight behind the claims of the English King, Henry VI.

Joan grew up during this period of civil war and invasion and once her village was evacuated when the English army marched through. Little is known about her childhood days. She had two older brothers and a younger brother and sister. She was never taught to read or write but spent much of her time listening to the village priest.

She soon became known as a very pious child, her favourite saints being St Catherine and St Michael. When she was sixteen, she began to have visions in which these saints came to speak with her. At first they merely told her to be good and go to church regularly; but later they began to say:

"You must go and fight for the King of France and bring peace to your country."

She kept the visions secret for a long time until the English began the siege of the important city of Orléans. Her voices became more and more insistent, telling her to go at once to the local military commander, M. de Baudricourt. "He will send you to the King and you will raise the siege of Orléans."

The reactions of her parents as soon as they learnt that Joan intended turning soldier were exactly as she had expected. Such a thing was totally unheard of and her father gave her a sound thrashing and threatened to drown her rather than let a daughter of his run off with a band of soldiers. Joan was not to be deterred, however, and she escaped from her parents' house and went to de Baudricourt.

It was not easy for an ordinary village girl to convince a hard-headed soldier that she had a divine mission to raise the siege of Orléans, a feat which seemed almost impossible to the military experts. The commander tried to send the girl back to her father but Joan continued to wait patiently on his doorstep asking to speak with him. Eventually de Baudricourt gave in and sent for the girl and listened to what she asked of him.

Although her honesty and simple determination impressed him he could not send her to the Dauphin's court without opening himself to ridicule from everyone who knew him. Joan answered all his logical arguments simply, finding common sense reasons for all of the things her voices had told her to do. Even her contempt for the French military tactics finally convinced him. Then, after she had told him of a heavy French defeat long before the official news reached him, de Baudricourt could no longer doubt that she had been sent by God.

He gave her the horse she asked for and the suit of men's

Roger Hart.

clothing, and sent her to the Dauphin with a letter and an escort of men-at-arms. News of the maid who was going to save France had preceded her to the court and already many different stories of miracles were being associated with her name. The Queen Mother brought her to the Dauphin where she repeated her message telling him that God was sending her to free his land from the invaders and to have him crowned rightful King of all France in Rheims Cathedral.

The Dauphin was a weak man who was easily swayed by his powerful and confident courtiers and who doubted his own ability. The quiet assurance of the maid seemed to give him new heart and for once he ignored his advisers who merely laughed at Joan's country manners and put her in charge of his army.

Joan was fitted out in armour and received a holy sword from behind the altar of the church of St Catherine at Tours. The army left for Orléans on 28 April 1429 at the beginning of one of the most remarkable military campaigns in history. Joan was able to persuade most of her chief officers that they had been fighting the wrong kind of war. She was determined to use the shock tactics and realistic, disciplined type of war that had been used by the English in their campaigns, rather than the knightly kind of game which the French were used to. If wars were worth fighting, she argued, they were worth fighting seriously to win at all costs.

With a small force of well-trained volunteers, Joan surprised the English and entered the besieged city at night when forces usually stopped fighting. Inside, she sent a message to the English commander:

"Give to the Maid, sent by God, the keys of all the cities you have taken in France and return to your own country where you belong."

Joan had never been described as beautiful but she had a striking face, and the sight of her in her shining armour with her white banner and quiet assurance so inspired the soldiers in Orléans that they were ready to rush out of the city and attack the enemy. But Joan made sure of her position and brought into play the newly-invented artillery. She sent word to the rest of her army waiting beyond the English forts surrounding the city and ten days after entering the city she led a violent attack on the English. Her plan worked perfectly; the surprised English were caught between the two groups of French troops, for those outside the city had attacked at exactly the same moment. The enemy were forced to abandon the siege and to retreat up the river Loire. They were forced from all their strongholds along the river and a month later a relief English army was totally routed by the French.

Joan became known as the Maid of Orléans and her victory was greeted with wild enthusiasm throughout France, Along with the story of her deeds went accounts of miracles and great wonders. Her next move was to have the Dauphin crowned as Charles VII. With the Dauphin at its head followed by Joan in her armour, the army marched through previously hostile lands to Rheims. In all the towns the people paid homage to the Dauphin and to Joan and the procession entered the city of Rheims in triumph. The coronation itself took place in the cathedral and was a tremendous political success. To try and stem the growing tide of French support, the English brought the boy King Henry VI to France and had him crowned King of France in Paris.

Now that Joan's immediate objective had been achieved, Charles VII and his advisers wanted to make a peace treaty with the English who had made their headquarters at the city of Rouen. The Maid, however, wanted to keep on fighting until the English were forced to return to England. With quarrels now in her army she marched towards Paris to relieve that city. In September she had her first sense of failure when an attack on Paris was beaten off, Joan herself being wounded. Charles immediately withdrew his army and paid them off for the winter months ahead.

Joan refused to spend the winter at court and, with a tiny band of her faithful soldiers, she laid siege to another of the English strongholds. The next spring she rejoined the main army to relieve the key fortress of Compiènge which was besieged by the Burgundians. Another of her surprise raids succeeded in forcing entry to the city. Then the same evening she led an attack out of the town during which she was dragged from her horse and taken prisoner by the Burgundians.

Joan's successes had caused many influential people to hate her and her refusal to attend the winter court had annoyed the King himself. Therefore the Maid's enemies were able to persuade Charles not to pay the ransom money demanded by the Burgundians for Joan's release.

The English were quick to seize their opportunity and paid the £10,000 demanded for the Maid and in November 1430 she was brought to Rouen and locked in the military prison. She made one brave effort to escape by leaping out of the window of her tower but she was soon recaptured.

The English for political reasons let the Church put Joan on trial. The English churchmen prepared a list of sixty-four charges against her, including such things as flying through the air like a witch and of stealing a bishop's horse. The French Bishop Cauchon who was in charge of the trial had these charges reduced to the twelve most serious. Joan was put on trial for heresy in claiming that she had received direct messages from God and in wearing the clothes of a man. The Church believed that *it* was the only voice of God and therefore Joan was putting herself above the Church, an unforgivable sin.

Joan claimed that she had worn men's clothes because it was only common sense to do so when she had had to mix with men in all her work. And she continued to maintain that St Catherine and St Michael had indeed spoken to her. Her trial was as fair as any medieval trial, Bishop Cauchon attempting to make her confess her heresy and avoid the punishment of being burnt at the stake so openly that he was reprimanded by the English authorities. One of the young priests at the trial kept an account of the proceedings and it is from this fascinating historical document that most of our knowledge of Joan comes.

Joan had been told by her voices that she would be captured but would be freed. Thus when threatened with torture and shown the stake ready for her, she began to realise that this time at least her voices had been wrong and there was no escape. She signed the paper with her confession on it. In it she confessed to having been misled by voices of the devil and that she had blasphemed by wearing unnaturally the clothes of a man. All her other sins she renounced and swore to be obedient to the Holy Church.

But when Joan learned that, in spite of her recantation, she had been sentenced to life imprisonment by the Church court, she tore her confession to pieces and gave her most famous speech to her judges. She called them liars and bitterly regretted listening to their foolish promises. They had promised her life; did they not realise that to be shut away from the light, from the fields and the sky, from the churches where she prayed was far worse than death?

"I know now that yours are the voices of the devil. I will trust to the mercy of God."

As a relapsed heretic she was handed over to the Executioner to be burnt at the stake. In normal burnings of this kind the Executioner would climb up behind and strangle the victim as soon as there was enough smoke to hide him. In Joan's case the stake was made higher than usual and she would have to suffer the agonising death of fire.

On 30 May 1431 she was taken out of her prison and tied to the stake in the market-place. She showed no fear and asked only for someone to give her a cross to hold. The Churchmen refused but an English soldier gave her two pieces of stick. Her last words were to her confessor who begged her to confess to him even after the fire had been set alight. Joan quietly warned him to jump down before he, too, was caught in the flames.

Many of the crowd who had come to jeer were swayed by her courageous bearing and went away inspired by her nobility. The English breathed a sigh of relief now that they had done with the Maid of Orléans.

But Joan's memory remained alive in the hearts of the French. They had learnt from her ideas of war and within twenty years of her death the only part of France left in English hands was the coastal city of Calais.

Joan's story does not end there. Her brothers had been pressing for a retrial and Charles VII was at last forced to order one. At this inquiry in 1455 Joan was pardoned of the charge of heresy and her earlier judges declared full of corruption and malice. Finally in 1920, almost 500 years since her death at the age of twenty-one, Joan was canonised by the Roman Catholic Church as Saint Joan, the most famous warrior saint in the Church's calendar.

Discussion

a. Are people who claim to see visions and hear voices mad? Find out about other people who have seen visions.
b. Write an account of one of Joan's victories from the point of view of one of her ordinary soldiers.
c. Joan believed in fighting wars to win at all cost. Do you agree with this? Does the same apply to sport?
d. What is a miracle? Do miracles ever happen today?
e. What is heresy? Should anybody or any organisation insist on people believing what is accepted as right?

f. Can a soldier also be a saint?
g. Find out about suffragettes. Are there any jobs that women cannot do as well as men? Why are there few women engineers?
h. Should a woman wear men's clothes? Does long hair indicate an effeminate person? What does the word *fashion* mean?

Use Your Imagination

a. Divide the class into four groups; each group take a man in this story who clashed with Joan. Write a scene which shows how Joan conflicts with the person and what results from the clash. Then put the scenes together and act it as a play.
b. Write an account of one of Joan's victories from the point-of-view of one of her ordinary soldiers.

AMY JOHNSON

Amy Johnson was born in Hull, England, in 1905. After completing her education she took a job in London, where she joined the London Aeroplane Club and in 1928 learned to fly.

This was the year in which Bert Hinkler became the first person to make a solo flight from England to Australia; it soon became Amy's ambition to become the first woman to fly alone to Australia. Despite her friends' insistence that such an attempt would be sure to end in disaster, she persisted in her plans and in 1930 she set off in an old de Havilland Gipsy Moth which she had bought for six hundred pounds.

Six days after leaving London she reached Karachi in India—a world record! A few days before she had been unknown; now the whole world was following her flight with interest.

Over Burma she encountered a violent tropical storm, and when forced to land near Rangoon damaged the undercarriage of her plane. The damage was quickly repaired, however, and she was off again, battling against heavy winds and torrential rains.

After an enthusiastic welcome at Singapore she set off on the most perilous part of her journey, across the Dutch East Indies and the shark-infested Timor Sea. When all contact with her plane was lost for twenty-four hours, it was feared that she had crashed, and ships were being sent out to search for her when the news came that she had reached Darwin safely. At Brisbane she made a faulty landing and so was unable to fly on to Sydney. By this time the whole world was applauding the courage of Amy Johnson, who had made the flight from England to Australia in nineteen days.

Amy made several other famous flights. In 1931 she flew from London to Tokyo and back; in 1932 she broke the record from London to Cape Town, making the 7,000 mile journey in just over four days. In 1936 she again flew from London to Cape Town and back, breaking all existing records.

When war broke out in 1939 she joined the Air Transport Auxiliary Force. Her work now consisted of ferrying planes from factories to Air Force bases; it was on one of these flights in 1941 that her plane crashed in the Thames estuary and she was killed.

Discussion and Research

    a. Find out all you can about other famous women aviators, such as Jean Batten, Amelia Earhart.

    b. Should women be allowed to become astronauts? Find out what you can about the Russian woman cosmonaut.

Use Your Imagination

    Imagine that you are flying alone above the jungle when you encounter a tremendous rain storm. Describe your experiences.

WAR DIARY

(Anne Frank was one of eight people, all Jews, who lived for two years in the hiding place they called their *Secret Annexe*, at the back of an office building and warehouse in Amsterdam. They had chosen to hide from the Germans rather than be sent to a concentration camp. Anne had just turned thirteen when they went into hiding and she died in a German concentration camp two months short of her sixteenth birthday. Until her family was found by the Gestapo, Anne kept a diary of her activities, hopes and feelings. The diary was discovered after the war and became a bestseller).

Tuesday, 20 *October* 1942

Dear Kitty,

My hand still shakes, although it's two hours since we had the shock. I should explain that there are five fire-extinguishers in the house. We knew that someone was coming to fill them, but no one had warned us when the carpenter, or whatever you call him, was coming.

The result was that we weren't making any attempt to keep quiet, until I heard hammering outside on the landing opposite our bookcase door. I thought of the carpenter at once and warned Elli, who was having a meal with us, that she shouldn't go downstairs. Daddy and I posted ourselves at the door so as to hear when the man left. After he'd been working for a quarter of an hour, he laid his hammer and tools down on top of our cupboard (as we thought) and knocked on the door. We turned absolutely white. Perhaps he had heard something after all and wanted to investigate our secret den. It seemed like it. The knocking, pulling, pushing, and wrenching went on. I nearly fainted at the thought that this utter stranger might discover our beautiful secret hiding-place. And just as I thought my last hour was at hand, I heard Mr Koophuis say, "Open the door, it's only me." We opened immediately. The hook that holds the cupboard, which can be undone by people who know the secret, had got jammed. That was why no one had been able to warn us about the carpenter. The man had now gone downstairs and Koophuis wanted to fetch Elli, but couldn't open the bookcase again. It was a great relief to me, I can tell you. In my imagination the man who I thought was trying to get in had been growing and growing in size until in the end he appeared to be a giant and the greatest Fascist that ever walked the earth.

Yours,

Anne

Tuesday, 13 *July* 1943

Dear Kitty,

Yesterday afternoon, with Daddy's permission, I asked Dussel whether he would please be so good (being really very polite) as to allow me to use the little table in our room twice a week in the afternoons, from four o'clock till half-past five. I sit there every day from half-past two till four, while Dussel sleeps, but

otherwise the room plus table are out of bounds. Inside, in our common room, there is much too much going on; it is impossible to work there and besides, Daddy likes to sit at the writing-table and work too sometimes.

So it was quite a reasonable request, and the question was put very politely. Now honestly what do you think the very learned Dussel replied: "No!" Just plain "No!" I was indignant and refused to be put off like that, so I asked him the reason for his "No". But I was sent away with a flea in my ear. This was the barrage which followed:

"I have to work too, and if I can't work in the afternoons then there is no time left for me at all. I must finish my task, otherwise I've started it all for nothing. Anyway, you don't work seriously at anything. Your mythology, now just what kind of work is that? Knitting and reading are not work either. I am at the table and shall stay there."

My reply was: "Mr Dussel, I do work seriously and there is nowhere else for me to work in the afternoons. I beg of you to kindly reconsider my request!"

With these words the offended Anne turned her back on the very learned doctor, ignoring him completely. I was seething with rage, and thought Dussel frightfully rude (which he jolly well was) and myself very friendly. In the evening when I could get hold of Pim, I told him how it had gone off and discussed what I should do next, because I was not going to give in, and preferred to clear it up myself. Pim told me how I ought to tackle the problem, but warned me that it would be better to leave it till the next day, as I was so het up. I let this go to the winds, and waited for Dussell after washing-up. Pim sat in the room next to us, which had a calming influence on me. I began: "Mr Dussel, I don't suppose you see any point in discussing the matter any more, but I must ask you to do so." Dussel then remarked with his sweetest smile: "I am always, and at all times, prepared to discuss this matter, but it has already been settled."

I went on talking, though continually interrupted by Dussel. "When you first came here we arranged that this room should be for both of us; if we were to divide it fairly, you would have the morning and I all the afternoon! But I don't even ask that much, and I think that my two afternoons are really perfectly reasonable." At this Dussel jumped up as if someone had stuck a needle into him. "You can't talk about your rights here at all.

And where am I to go, then? I shall ask Mr Van Daan whether he will build a little compartment in the attic, then I can go and sit there. I simply can't work anywhere. With you one always gets trouble. If your sister Margot, who after all has more reason to ask such a thing, would have come to me with the same questions, I would not think of refusing, but you . . . " Then followed the business about the mythology and the knitting, and Anne was insulted again. However, she did not show it and let Dussel finish speaking: "But you, one simply can't talk to you. You are outrageously selfish, as long as you can get what you want, you don't mind pushing everyone else to one side, I've never met such a child. But after all, I suppose I shall be told later that Anne Frank failed her exam because Mr Dussel would not give up the table for her."

It went on and on and finally it was such a torrent I could hardly keep pace with it. At one moment I thought, "In a minute I'll give him such a smack in the face that he'll fly up to the ceiling together with his lies," but the next moment I said to myself, "Keep calm! Such a fellow isn't worth getting worked up about."

After giving vent to his fury, Master Dussel left the room with an expression of mixed wrath and triumph, his coat stuffed with food. I dashed to Daddy and told him all that he had not already heard of the story. Pim decided to talk to Dussel the same evening, which he did. They talked for over half an hour. The theme of the conversation was something like this: first of all they talked about whether Anne should sit at the table, yes or no. Daddy said that he and Dussel had already discussed the subject once before, when he had professed to agree with Dussel, in order not to put him in the wrong in front of the young. But Daddy had not thought it fair then. Dussel thought that I should not speak as if he was an intruder who tried to monopolise everything, but Daddy stuck up for me firmly over that, because he had heard for himself that I had not breathed a word of such a thing.

To and fro it went, Daddy defending my selfishness and my *trifling* work, Dussel grumbling continually.

Finally, Dussel had to give in after all, and I had the opportunity of working undisturbed until five o'clock for two afternoons a week. Dussel looked down his nose very much, didn't speak to me for two days and still had to go and sit at the table from five till half-past—frightfully childish.

A person of fifty-four who is still so pedantic and small-minded must be so by nature, and will never improve.

Yours,

Anne

Friday, 29 *October* 1943

Dear Kitty,

There have been resounding rows again between Mr and Mrs Van Daan. It came about like this: as I have already told you, the Van Daans are at the end of their money. One day, some time ago now, Koophuis spoke about a furrier with whom he was on good terms: this gave Van Daan the idea of selling his wife's fur coat. It's a fur coat made from rabbit skins, and she has worn it seventeen years. He got 325 florins for it—an enormous sum. However, Mrs Van Daan wanted to keep the money to buy new clothes after the war, and it took some doing before Mr Van Daan made it clear to her that the money was urgently needed for the household.

The yells and screams, stamping and abuse—you can't possibly imagine it! It was frightening. My family stood at the bottom of the stairs, with bated breath, ready if necessary to drag them apart! All this shouting and weeping and nervous tension are so unsettling and such a strain, that in the evening I drop into my bed crying, thanking heaven that I sometimes have half an hour to myself.

All goes well with me on the whole, except that I have no appetite. I keep being told: "You don't look at all well." I must say they are doing their very best to keep me up to the mark. Grape sugar, cod liver oil, yeast tablets, and calcium have all been lined up.

My nerves often get the better of me: it is especially on Sundays that I feel rotten. The atmosphere is so oppressive, and sleepy and as heavy as lead. You don't hear a single bird outside, and a deadly close silence hangs everywhere, catching hold of me as if it will drag me down into an underworld.

At such times Daddy, Mummy, and Margot leave me cold. I wander from one room to another, downstairs and up again, feeling like a song-bird whose wings have been brutally clipped and who is beating itself in utter darkness against the bars of its cage. "Go outside, laugh, and take a breath of fresh air," a voice cries within me, but I don't even feel a response any more;

I go and lie on the divan and sleep, to make the time pass more quickly, and the stillness and the terrible fear, because there is no way of killing them.

Yours,

Anne

Discussion

a. What is a *race* or a *nation* of people? Are there any differences between races? Why did the Germans persecute the Jews in the last war?

b. What is *prejudice*? Are there any kinds of racial prejudices left in the world today? What has caused them?

c. Anne says that *her nerves* often got the better of her. What does she mean by that? Are girls any more nervous than boys? Do girls cry more than boys? Why?

d. Do people need to be alone sometimes? What happens when people are shut up together for any length of time, e.g. a wet weekend?

e. Is it natural for parents to quarrel? Should the man be the head of the family?

Use Your Imagination

a. Write Dussel's account of his quarrel with Anne about the use of the table.

b. Using factual information, where possible, write the diary of a black African in South Africa or a black in a southern town in the United States of America.

c. Write a short story or play about a situation where everybody gets on everybody's nerves.

d. If you were not allowed to leave your room for two years, what would you want to have and how would you occupy your time?

MONSTERS

Theseus

Perseus and Medusa

THE DEATH
of
THE DRAGON

YETI

Beowulf

Out of the Sea

Minotaur

Exploring the Theme

1. Discuss the use of *monster* in the following:
   i. There is a *monster* sale at this store today.
   ii. He's not a man—he's a *monster*.
   iii. This is *monstrous* behaviour, and I'll have no more of it.
   iv. What a *monster* of a baby.
   v. The *Monster* from Outer Space.
2. Do you believe in the Yeti (The Abominable Snowman) or the Loch Ness Monster? Do you believe in UFOs (Unidentified Flying Objects)?

3. How do you account for the fact that every country, independently in many cases, has myths about monsters and giants?
4. What has Science Fiction to do with monsters?
5. Why do you think the dragon occurs so widely in mythology, e.g. in China as well as England?
6. Find out what you can about the following monsters: chimera, griffin, sphinx, leviathon, Gargantua. Add to this list.

THESEUS AND THE MINOTAUR

A GREEK HERO AND MONSTER

On a visit to Corinth, King Aegus of Athens secretly married the Princess Aethra. She had grown tired of waiting for her promised husband to come home from Lydia. When it was time for King Aegus to leave Corinth he said to Aethra, "I am afraid I must leave you now. It will be safest if you have a son, to pretend that his father is the god Poseidon. My brothers and nephews would certainly try and kill the boy if they found out about our marriage. My eldest nephew expects to be the next king of Athens."

Aethra had a son whom she called Theseus and on his fourteenth birthday she asked him: "Can you move that huge rock?" Theseus lifted it easily and tossed it aside. Hidden underneath he found a sword with a golden snake pattern inlaid on the blade and also a pair of sandals.

"Those were left there by your father," Aethra told him. "He is Aegus, King of Athens. Take them to him and say that you found them under this rock, but be careful not to say anything to your cousins who will try to kill you if they find out you are the true heir to the throne of Athens. It is because of them I have always pretended that your father was Poseidon."

Theseus eagerly buckled on both sword and sandals and set out overland on his dangerous journey to Athens. He had not gone far before he met one, Periphetes the Clubman, a lame bandit who was the terror of all travellers on this road. What he lacked in his legs he made up for in the strength of his arms. His only weapon was a tremendous club shod with iron which was death to all who did not hand over all their valuables. Theseus showed his great strength when he simply wrested the club from the brigand's hands and treated him in the same way as he had treated so many passers-by.

This became the method that Theseus always adopted with evil-doers of all sorts; for next he dealt with Sinis the Pinebender, whose great delight was to bend two pine trees down towards each other, tying some poor unfortunate traveller to their tops by his arms and then suddenly letting go of the trees. The trees would, of course, fly upright and tear the victim in two. This notorious ruffian greeted Theseus as he approached:

"Stranger, come and test your strength by helping me bend down this pine tree!"

But Theseus knew what to expect and when the tree was bent down it was he, not Sinis, who let go first and sent his partner flying through the air. Wasting no time, Theseus tied him to two pine trees and treated him exactly as he had treated others.

Next Theseus killed a monstrous wild sow with tusks larger and sharper than sickles. Then as he was walking along a narrow rocky path at the top of some high cliffs that fell away with a sheer drop into the sea, he met Sciron. "If you wish to pass along this way you must pay a toll!" he called out to Theseus. "Down on your knees and wash my feet."

Theseus knelt down as far from the cliff edge as he could and waited for Sciron to come towards him.

"And when you've washed my feet, you can then go and feed my turtle," called Sciron again. Theseus knew what this meant and as the brute came up to him he caught Sciron by the leg and flung him over his shoulder shouting:

"Go and feed the turtle yourself." Sciron went head first into the sea.

Continuing along the coast road, Theseus was stopped by another famous brigand, Cercyon, who wrestled with all comers and crushed their bones in his bearlike hug. But this time he met a man stronger than himself and in a short time he lay on his back with his ribs broken.

That same evening Theseus came to a solitary inn standing beside the road. "Good evening to you, stranger!" cried the inn-keeper who was called Procrustes. "You must be weary after a day's travel; come in and rest for the night. All travellers come to partake of my hospitality and to try my wonderful bed. You've heard of the Bed of Procrustes, no doubt? No? . . . well, you've a lot to learn. It's a magic bed and it fits anyone, great or small, long or short."

An old servant, the only one who really fitted the bed warned

the youth what to expect. To ensure that the bed really did fit everybody, Procrustes would stretch those who were too short on the rack; and he would cut off feet and legs if his guests were too tall. Theseus overpowered his host when bed-time came and fitted him on the bed that had seen the deaths of so many travellers. Theseus had to cut off the feet of Procrustes; but finding him still too tall, he cut off his head as well, wrapped the dead body in a blanket and flung it into the sea.

Thus, having made the road much safer for ordinary travellers, Theseus strode into Athens in search of his father. The King's new wife, a witch called Medea, knew by magic who he was and suggested to the young man that he capture the Cretan Bull which was laying waste the countryside, in order to prove his identity. This was the same animal which Hercules had brought from Crete and which Eurystheus had allowed to escape. Medea had no wish to see a new heir to the throne gain influence over the old king, and she was sure that Theseus would either be killed or else would be unable to perform the task and therefore not return to Athens. When, however, Theseus soon returned dragging the terrible beast by the horns, Medea realised the strength of the youth and determined to poison him as soon as possible.

At a feast to celebrate the capture of the Bull, Aegus saw the sword of the young hero and recognised it. Just as Theseus was about to drink of the poisoned cup which Medea had carefully prepared for him, the King dashed the cup to the floor where the poison burnt a large hole in the stone. Aegus sent to Corinth to fetch Theseus's mother and announced, "Theseus is my son and heir."

As soon as the nephews of Aegus heard this they raised an army and marched on Athens, meaning to kill this newcomer. Theseus, however, armed the Athenians, marched out of the city to meet the oncoming army, ambushed them, and massacred them.

He returned to Athens the next day to discover to his great surprise that the city was in mourning. To his questions the King replied that the envoys from Crete had arrived to collect their tribute of seven youths and maidens which they claimed every ninth year, and took back to Crete to feed the Minotaur. This monster, half bull, half man, was kept by Minos, King of Crete, in the Labyrinth or maze built under his palace at Knossos.

The tribute had been forced some years earlier when a son of King Minos had been murdered by Aegus's nephews during the Athletic Games in Athens.

As soon as Theseus had heard the whole story he exclaimed, "I will go as one of the youths and try my luck with this Minotaur. If I can slay it there will be no need for further tribute."

Although King Aegus did his best to dissuade his new-found son and heir from doing anything so foolhardy, Theseus was determined and set sail on the tribute ship with its black sails. Theseus told his father that if he returned alive having killed the Minotaur he would hoist white sails to give them all the news.

With a fair breeze the ship reached Crete in no time and its occupants were taken to the Royal Palace at Knossos. Here the victims were entertained and took part in athletic games. Theseus won all the competitions—running, jumping, wrestling, boxing and throwing the discus—and became the idol of, not only the people of Crete, but also Ariadne, the King's daughter, who fell in love with the accomplished Athenian prince.

She went secretly to Theseus that night with a ball of thread and told him her plan. "No one has ever found his way out of the Labyrinth but take this thread with you when your turn comes and fasten it to the door when it is closed after you, so you can find your way back. I will come to the door at midnight to let you out. You will have to take me with you for I will not be welcome here when the King finds out I have helped you."

Theseus was the first of the Athenians to be chosen for sacrifice and he followed Ariadne's instructions very carefully. He wandered through the maze of caverns until at length he came to the centre chamber where the Minotaur lived. It was a fearsome and hideous creature with a great human body and the neck and head of a bull. When it saw Theseus it rushed upon him bellowing with rage and hunger. Theseus, of course, had no weapon; but as the creature reached him he smote it over the heart with his fist and then leapt nimbly aside. Bellowing more fiercely than ever the Minotaur turned and charged at him again; and again Theseus smote it and leapt aside. Again and again he did this to the maddened creature until it began to weaken. Finally Theseus seized it by the horns and forced back its head until with a mighty crack the neck broke and the Minotaur lay dead.

After resting a little Theseus picked up the end of the thread and retraced his steps to the door where, true to her word,

Ariadne was waiting for him. Swiftly she led him and the other Athenians to their ship and, while it was still dark, they crept on board, cut the cables, and stole silently out of the harbour.

Theseus beached his ship on the island of Naxos because he was in need of food and water. While Ariadne was wandering by the shore, the god Dionysus saw her and fell in love with her. He cast her into a deep sleep and appeared to Theseus in a dream saying, "I want to marry Ariadne. If you don't leave the island at once, I will destroy Athens by sending all its people mad."

There was nothing for Theseus to do but abandon Ariadne and return to Athens. In his haste to reach home again he forgot all about his promise to his father and did not change the sails to white. King Aegus, watching anxiously from the cliff for the return of his son, saw the black sail appear and, believing his son dead, he threw himself into the sea and was drowned.

Theseus became King of Athens in his father's place and ruled his people well, although he was too adventurous to stay home quietly. There are many stories of his later mighty deeds but unfortunately there is no room for them here.

Discussion

a. How can a young boy today prove he's a man? By turning twenty-one?

b. Do you believe in tit-for-tat, revenge, an eye for an eye, or, turning the other cheek?

c. Find out about the history of the Olympic Games. What prospects do you think there are for international sport?

d. The Minotaur of Crete is seen as half bull, half man. The most popular sport of the Cretans seems to have been bull-fighting or at least bull-leaping. How does this help to explain the origins of the legend?

Use Your Imagination

a. Write Ariadne's story, as she might have told it.

b. Prepare a modern dance version, with mime and narration by a chorus, of the main Theseus story.

c. Write another adventure for Theseus.

d. Write a poem written by the King before he threw himself into the sea.

PERSEUS AND MEDUSA

ANOTHER GREEK HERO AND MONSTER

An oracle had warned Acrisius, King of Argos, that his grandson would kill him. "Then I shall take good care to have no grandchildren," Acrisius grunted.

He immediately locked his only daughter Danaë in a tower with solid brass doors guarded by a savage dog and brought all her food with his own hands.

But Zeus fell in love with Danaë when he saw her leaning sadly over the high balcony of the tower. To disguise himself from his wife Hera, Zeus became a shower of golden rain and descended on the tower. Danaë hurried inside, the rain trickling after her and then Zeus changed himself back into human shape and asked the girl to marry him.

A son was born to her and she called him Perseus. When Acrisius heard a baby crying behind the brass door he became filled with anger and fear. "Who is your husband?" he demanded.

"The god Zeus, Father," she replied, "and if you dare touch your grandchild, Zeus will immediately strike you dead."

Acrisius refused to believe his daughter and said that someone must have stolen away the key and married Danaë in secret. He was, however, not willing to risk the possibility that Danaë was telling the truth. Instead of killing the two he locked them in a huge wooden chest, with nothing more than a basket of food and a bottle of wine, and threw the chest into the sea. "If they drown," he said, "it will be the fault of Poseidon, God of the Sea, not mine."

Zeus knew what was happening and ordered Poseidon to take particular care of the chest. The baby slept on and Danaë prayed continually to Zeus for help. The chest floated gently on the sea all night and in the morning it was discovered by a fisherman from the island of Seriphos who caught it with his net and towed it ashore. When he knocked the top off the chest, out stepped Danaë, carrying the baby in her arms.

The kindly fisherman, whose name was Dictys, took them to his own home and looked after them. There Perseus grew up into a strong and noble youth learning all the skills of combat and defence that Dictys could teach him.

At length the king of the island, Polydectes, heard of the two and sent to have them brought to his own palace. Immediately he fell in love with the beautiful Danaë but she would not marry him because she had been the wife of Zeus. Polydectes could not take Danaë by force because he was afraid of the strength of young Perseus. He therefore decided on a strategem which would remove the youth. He held a huge feast to which he invited all the young men of the island, including Perseus. When all the guests arrived they brought magnificent gifts to the King. Perseus alone had nothing to bring and the other young men began to mock him about his poverty and obscure birth.

Perseus in his humiliation swore that he would bring any gift the King desired. Polydectes promptly spoke out, "All I want is the head of Medusa the Gorgon." To the laughter of all the guests, Perseus rushed out of the hall determined to bring the King what he wanted or die in the attempt.

Medusa had once been a beautiful woman, but, for defiling the temple of Athene, she had been turned into a gorgon, a hideous winged monster with a horrible face, huge teeth, and snakes for hair. She was said to be completely invulnerable because whoever looked at her face was turned into stone.

Perseus wandered along the seashore as he pondered over what to do to begin his impossible task. Suddenly he was startled by the appearance of two of the Immortals before him: Athene, tall and stately in her shining helmet and the polished shield on her arm; and Hermes, slim and quick with the winged sandals on his feet. "Do not grieve, Perseus," said Hermes, "for Zeus, your father, has sent us to help you. Here is the sharpest sword in the world."

"And here," said Athene, "is my polished shield. If you look at the gorgon's reflection in the shield, you will be able to cut off her head in safety."

Hermes continued, "Leave your mother; she will be safe with Dictys until you return. And go quickly to the north and visit the Grey Sisters. From them you will learn how to find the Naiads of the North who will give you everything else you need."

Perseus was left alone on the seashore. Quickly he made up his mind, and following Hermes' instructions, he came to the cave of the three Grey Sisters who had been born old women with grey hair. The three sisters had but one eye and tooth between them and Perseus was able to snatch the precious eye as they were passing it from one to another. Despite their cries he refused to return the eye until they gave him directions to the magic land behind the north wind where the Naiads lived.

When he had learnt what he wanted, he returned the eye and continued his journey. He was welcomed kindly by the Naiads and would have stayed long in that beautiful country if it had not been for his urgent quest. The Naiads gave Perseus the Shoes of Swiftness in order to escape from Medusa's winged sisters; they gave him also a magic bag in which to put the head; and finally one of the Naiads, a friend of Queen Proserpine, went down into the Underworld and borrowed the helmet of Hades which could make its wearer invisible.

Perseus thanked the Naiads and set out on the final stage of his quest—to the home of the Gorgons. Wearing the helmet and the sandals, he flew unseen to the island where they lived. All over the countryside he saw the statues of men and animals which had been living creatures until turned to stone by the gorgons.

At last he came upon the three terrible sisters lying asleep in the sun with the snakes which grew instead of hair, writhing about their heads. Medusa and her sisters were even more hideous than Perseus had expected. As well as the snakes they had white tusks like those of pigs and their bodies were covered with dragon-scales.

Perseus approached cautiously and, looking only at the reflection in Athene's shield, he lifted the sword Hermes had given him and cut off the horrible head at one blow. Then as quickly as possible—it was rather difficult looking at the image in the shield—he picked the head up and dropped it into the bag the Naiads had given him.

But the hissing of the snakes was enough to wake Medusa's two sisters who sprang up in a terrible rage when they realised someone was attacking them. Luckily for Perseus the Shoes of Swiftness enabled him to outdistance his pursuers.

That was not the end of this adventure, however, for as he was flying home, he noticed a beautiful young woman chained to a rock on the edge of the sea. He swooped down to find out the cause of her distress, and learnt that her name was Andromeda and that her foolish mother had offended the sea nymphs who had sent a monster to ravage all the coasts of the kingdom ruled by Andromeda's father. Hoping to appease the monster, her parents had chained her there as a sacrifice. Perseus released the beautiful girl with whom he had fallen deeply in love, and waited until the monster came swimming near the rock. When it was close to him, he drew the head of Medusa out of its bag and held it in front of the monster. It sank back into the water, cold and lifeless, a long ridge of jagged stone which exists to this day.

Perseus then went to Andromeda's father to ask for her hand in marriage. The King refused to allow his daughter to marry an unknown stranger and said that she had been promised to a foreign prince, the son of the King of Tyre. Andromeda did not like the prince and when he tried to take her away by force, Perseus whispered to Andromeda to close her eyes, and pulled Medusa's head from its bag again. Everyone was turned to stone and Perseus picked Andromeda up in his arms and flew back home with her to Seriphos.

Here he found that Dictys had been thrown into prison while his mother Danaë had been made a slave in the household of Polydectes. Perseus left Andromeda outside and strode into the hall of the King who was feasting with the same band of youths who had jeered at him before.

When Polydectes scornfully asked for the head of the gorgon, Perseus deliberately drew it from the bag and turned the whole company into stone. The stone lumps which had once been men were dragged out and left on the hillside and Perseus set Dictys as king over the island. Danaë married this good man with the approval of Zeus.

Before leaving the island Perseus gave back his shield to Athene and asked Hermes to return the things he had borrowed from the Naiads. He also gave the head of Medusa to Athene who set it in the centre of her shield.

Perseus and Andromeda sailed from the island for Argos where his grandfather was still king. While the vessel was in port at a neighbouring city, however, Perseus took part in some athletic games which were being held there. Perseus distinguished himself in all events and in the discus throw he hurled the iron disc so hard that it struck a member of the crowd of spectators killing him instantly. This turned out to be none other than Perseus' grandfather, Acrisius, who was a visitor to the games. Thus the prophecy was fulfilled.

Perseus married Andromeda, became King in place of his grandfather and lived a long and happy life.

Discussion
   a. What does the slang phrase, *passing the buck* mean?
   b. Will it make any difference to your life if you have this, or that, kind of parents?
   c. Relate some unusual coincidences you have experienced or heard about.

Use Your Imagination
   a. Take an unusual rock formation, or other physical feature you know well, and imagine a myth which accounts for its shape and position.
   b. Write about *The Coincidence That Wasn't.*
   c. Make a clay model, drawing, or painting of Medusa's head.
   d. Poverty.
   e. Look at the painting *The Rescue of Andromeda* by Piero di Cosimo.

BEOWULF AND THE DRAGON

FROM AN OLD ENGLISH EPIC

Then the hero, stern under his gleaming helmet,
With his stout mailcoat and thick-plated shield,
Strode out to meet his foe. Toward the mound he moved,
The rock rampart cleft with arch of stone. Close by,
Strongly from the earth gushed out a stream, whose wash,
Boiled to fury in the dragon's furnace breath,
Dropped to the steamy ground so scalding fierce,
So hissing-hot that Beowulf could tread no farther.
He halted—in a loud voice he shouted his battle cry.
Then the dragon awoke. Crackling, he uncurled; like the clash
Of shield upon shield, he uncurled his scaly length;
With thunderclapping sound he twisted through the arch,
Spitting flame. He blackened the rampart, he scorched
And burnt the grass, as round and round madly
He bounded upon the bruised ground. Then Beowulf,
Wreathed in smoke and fire, ran upon the dragon;
Shielded, brandishing his sword, he struck him mightily—

The keen edge bit on the scales and glanced aside,
But roused his dreadful wrath, Uprearing, he flapped
Wide his monstrous wings, fanning the blaze
Tenfold; like a forest fire, tree-ravenous, devouring
All in its path, he bore down on the pygmy king,
Till Beowulf, choked in that frenzy of smoke and flame,
Scarce could breathe . . . he stumbled . . . he gasped for air . . .

Then the warriors, his friends on the headland, chieftain's sons
Whom he himself had chosen, when they saw their King
Sore-pressed, his strength waning, forsook him—
In terror for their lives they took to the woods, all
But Wiglaf, close kinsman of the King, whose spirit,
Fashioned in stronger mould, cried out that his master
Should thus suffer. His hand seized the shield,
The frail linden wood; he drew his sword,
Proud heirloom of his fathers, and called to his comrades: "Stay,
Fellow warriors! The King needs us, now
As never before. Is this the time to desert him?
Have you forgotten the gifts he gave us in the mead hall
When we feasted together—the gold rings, the shields
And flashing swords? Have you forgotten that solemnly
We swore to protect him from peril? Us alone
He chose for this venture, named us of all spearmen
The bravest. Turn now, O my comrades, and fight!"
But they shrank from his chiding and cringed among the trees.
Then cried he in torment of soul: "Shame upon you!
Do your coward hearts knock at your ribs so loud
You cannot hear me? Or do you not wish to hear?
Is your master no more to you than carcass meat
For monsters? I'd rather my body were burnt to a cinder
Than stand by to see him slain. For him be my hand now,
My helmet, my sword, my mailcoat—all for him!"
And he called into the smoke and fire, "Beloved King,
Whose name is known in the farthest corners of the earth,
Wherever the ocean laps the windy shore
And the wave-worn headland, remember the boast of your youth—
Never to yield, never to fail in striving.
Wake the old might of your hands!" He plunged into the smoke
Until he stood where he loved best to be—
By his master's side. In the whiplash and flogging of flame

Steadfast together they fought. Between the King
And the fiery dragon he thrust his linden shield—
The lightning licked it, shrivelled it up like shavings
Thrown to the fire. Then might Wiglaf have perished,
But Beowulf housed him under his iron shield
And, rousing his old might, raised high the sword
And struck the dragon. Too strong was the hand—the steel
Was shivered to pieces. With savage haste the dragon,
Old twilight foe, in whirlwind conflagration
Rushed upon him. Deep into his neck he plunged
His spiked teeth—the life-blood spurted, welled
Red over his armour. Then Wiglaf, as love for his lord
Flashed into rage, unshielded sprang at the beast.
Into that fiery furnace he thrust his sword,
With scorched fingers drove it under the scales,
Home to the hilt. And the dragon fell back, his breathing
Laboured, the fire-puffs ponderous and slow. Then Beowulf,
Master of his waning might, drew from his mailcoat
His keen battle-knife; locked in combat with the foe,
He struck at the heart. So smiting, with Wiglaf he felled him;
Together they quenched the fire, together beat out
His loathsome life. O valiant, valiant knight,
Who at King's peril never did falter! Such
Should a warrior strive to be.

Discussion

   a. In what ways is the monster made frightening? Why should
      dragons breathe smoke and fire?
   b. What qualities of the hero are represented by Beowulf and
      Wiglaf?
   c. What is the difference between honour and loyalty?
   d. What things do you honour? What do you feel loyal
      towards? Why?
   e. Would you ever be a martyr for something you believed in?
   f. Is anger always bad?

Use Your Imagination

   a. Write a story entitled, *And His Friends Forsook Him.*
   b. Write a story entitled, *A Friend in Need.*
   c. Write a poem by one of the warriors who deserted Beowulf.

THE DEATH OF THE DRAGON

FROM *THE HOBBIT*

(The people of Esgaroth have seen a great light appear at the end of the lake near the Lonely Mountain. At first they think the King beneath the Mountain has returned and there is great excitement.)

There was once more a tremendous excitement and enthusiasm. But the grim-voiced fellow ran hotfoot to the Master, "The dragon is coming or I am a fool!" he cried. "Cut the bridge! To arms! To arms!"

Then warning trumpets were suddenly sounded, and echoed along the rocky shores. The cheering stopped and the joy was turned to dread. So it was that the dragon did not find them unprepared.

Before long, so great was his speed, they could see him as a spark of fire rushing towards them and growing ever huger and more bright, and not the most foolish doubted that the prophecies had gone rather wrong. Still they had a little time. Every vessel in the town was filled with water, every warrior was armed, every arrow and dart was ready, and the bridge to the land was thrown down and destroyed, before the roar of Smaug's terrible approach grew loud, and the lake rippled red as fire beneath the awful beating of his wings.

Amid shrieks and shouts of men he came over them, swept towards the bridge and was foiled! The bridge was gone, and his enemies were on an island in deep water—too deep and dark and cool for his liking. If he plunged into it, a vapour and a steam would arise enough to cover all the land with a mist for days; but the lake was mightier than he, it would quench him before he could pass through.

Roaring he swept back over the town. A hail of dark arrows leaped up and snapped and rattled on his scales and jewels, and their shafts fell back kindled by his breath burning and hissing into the lake. No fireworks you ever imagined equalled the sights that night. At the twanging of the bows and the shrilling of the trumpets the dragon's wrath blazed to its height, till he was blind and mad with it. No one had dared to give battle to him for many an age; nor would they have dared now, if it had not been for the grim-voiced man (Bard was his name), who ran to and fro cheering on the archers and urging the Master to order them to fight to the last arrow.

Fire leaped from the dragon's jaws. He circled for a time high in the air above them, lighting all the lake; the trees by the shores shone like copper and like blood with leaping shadows of dense black at their feet. Then down he swooped straight through the arrow-storm, reckless in his rage, taking no heed to turn his scaly sides towards his foes, seeking only to set their town ablaze.

Fire leaped from thatched roofs and wooden beam-ends as he hurtled down and past and round again, though all had been drenched with water before he came. Once more water was flung by a hundred hands wherever a spark appeared. Back swirled the dragon. A sweep of his tail and the roof of the Great House crumbled and smashed down. Flames unquenchable sprang high into the night. Another swoop and another, and another house and then another sprang afire and fell; and still no arrow hindered Smaug or hurt him more than a fly from the marshes.

Already men were jumping into the water on every side. Women and children were being huddled into laden boats in the market pool. Weapons were flung down. There was mourning and weeping, where but a little time ago the old songs of mirth to come had been sung about the dwarfs. Now men cursed their names. The Master himself was turning to his great gilded boat, hoping to row away in the confusion and save himself. Soon all the town would be deserted and burned down to the surface of the lake.

That was the dragon's hope. They could all get into boats for all he cared. There he could have fine sport hunting them, or they could stop till they starved. Let them try to get to land and he would be ready. Soon he would set all the shoreland woods ablaze and wither every field and pasture. Just now he was enjoying the sport of town-baiting more than he had enjoyed anything for years.

But there was still a company of archers that held their ground among the burning houses. Their captain was Bard, grim-voiced and grim-faced, whose friends had accused him of prophesying floods and poisoned fish, though they knew his worth and courage. Now he shot with a great yew bow, till all his arrows but one were spent. The flames were near him. His companions were leaving him. He bent his bow for the last time.

Suddenly out of the dark something fluttered to his shoulder. He started—but it was only an old thrush. Unafraid it perched by his ear and brought him news. Marvelling he found he could understand its tongue, for he was of the race of Dale. "Wait! Wait!" it said to him. "The moon is rising. Look for the hollow of the left breast as he flies and turns above you!" And while Bard paused in wonder it told him of the tidings up in the Mountain and of all that it had heard.

Then Bard drew his bow-string to his ear. The dragon was circling back, flying low, and as he came the moon rose above the eastern shore and silvered his great wings.

"Arrow!" said the bowman. "Black arrow! I have saved you to the last. You have never failed me and always I have recovered you. I had you from my father and he from of old. If ever you came from the forges of the true king under the Mountain, go now and speed well!"

The dragon swooped once more lower than ever, and as he turned and dived down his belly glittered white with sparkling fires of gems in the moon—but not in one place. The great bow twanged. The black arrow sped straight from the string, straight for the hollow by the left breast where the foreleg was flung wide. In it smote and vanished, barb, shaft and feather, so fierce was its flight. With a shriek that deafened men, felled trees and split stone, Smaug shot spouting into the air, turned over and crashed down from on high in ruin.

Full on the town he fell. His last throes splintered it to sparks and gledes. The lake roared in. A vast steam leaped up, white in the sudden dark under the moon. There was a hiss, a gushing whirl and then silence. And that was the end of Smaug and Esgaroth, but not of Bard.

Discussion

    a. "The monster represents man's fears of the unknown and unknown dangers." How true is this of the dragon?

    b. Is the atomic bomb the twentieth century dragon?

Use Your Imagination

    a. Describe typical noises in one of these: hospital, cowshed, air terminal.

b. Describe typical noises in one of these: inside a stomach, at the centre of the earth, inside your mind.

c. Imagine that you live in a land where some of the beasts of fable really exist. Write entries for an encyclopaedia describing the appearance, habitat and food of some of the following: basilisk, chimera, dragon, griffin, hydra, manticora, phoenix.

d. Write the diary of a dragon.

OUT OF THE SEA

A MODERN SCIENCE FICTION MONSTER

(Michael and Phyllis Watson are journalists who have been sent to find out what has been attacking the coastal towns in the West Indies. Shipping has been attacked and now towns and it seems as if some alien civilisation has taken over the ocean deeps and is determined to exterminate all human beings. They are watching out of their hotel window.)

Then we had our first sight of a "sea-tank". A curve of dull grey metal sliding into the Square, carrying away the lower corner of a house front as it came.

Shots cracked at it from half a dozen different directions. The bullets splattered or thudded against it without effect. Slowly, heavily, with an air of inexorability, it came on, grinding and scraping across the cobbles. It was inclining slightly to its right, away from us and towards the church, carrying away more of the corner house, unaffected by the plaster, bricks, and beams that fell on it and slithered down its sides.

More shots smacked against it or ricochetted away whining, but it kept steadily on, thrusting itself into the Square at something under three miles an hour, massively undeflectible. Soon we were able to see the whole of it.

Imagine an elongated egg which has been halved down its length and set flat side to the ground, with the pointed end foremost. Consider this egg to be between thirty and thirty-five feet long, of a drab, lustreless colour, and you will have a fair picture of the *sea-tank* as we saw it pushing into the Square.

There was no way of seeing how it was propelled; there may have been rollers beneath, but it seemed, and sounded, simply to grate forward on its metal belly with plenty of noise, but none of machinery. It did not turn, as a tank does, but neither did it sheer like a car. It simply moved to the right on a diagonal, still pointing forwards. Close behind it followed another, exactly similar contrivance which slanted its way to the left, in our direction, wrecking the house front on the nearer corner of the street as it came. A third kept straight ahead into the middle of the Square, and then stopped.

At the far end, the crowd that had knelt about the priest scrambled to its feet, and fled. The priest himself stood his ground. He barred the thing's way. His right hand held a cross extended against it, his left was raised, fingers spread, and palm outward, to halt it. The thing moved on, neither faster nor slower, as if he had not been there. Its curved flank pushed him aside a little as it came. Then it, too, stopped.

A few seconds later the one up our end of the Square reached what was apparently its appointed position and also stopped.

"Troops will establish themselves at first objective in extended order," I said to Phyllis, as we regarded the three evenly spaced out in the Square. "This isn't haphazard. Now what?"

For half a minute it did not appear to be now anything. There was a little more sporadic shooting, some of it from windows which, all round the Square, were full of people hanging out to see what went on. None of it had any effect on the targets, and there was some danger from ricochets.

"Look!" said Phyllis suddenly. "This one's bulging."

She was pointing at the nearest. The previously smooth fore-and-aft sweep of its top was now disfigured at the highest point by a small, domelike excrescence. It was lighter-coloured than the metal beneath; a kind of off-white, semi-opaque substance which glittered viscously under the floods. It grew as one watched it.

"They're all doing it," she added.

There was a single shot. The excrescence quivered, but went on swelling. It was growing faster now. It was no longer dome-shaped, but spherical, attached to the metal by a neck, inflating like a balloon, and swaying slightly as it distended.

"It's going to pop. I'm sure it is," Phyllis said, apprehensively.

"There's another coming further down its back," I said. "Two more, look."

The first excrescence did not pop. It was already some two foot six in diameter and still swelling fast.

"It *must* pop soon," she muttered.

But still it did not. It kept on expanding until it must have been all of five feet in diameter. Then it stopped growing. It looked like a huge, repulsive bladder. A tremor and a shake passed through it. It jelly-wise, became detached, and wobbled into the air with the uncertainty of an overblown bubble.

In a lurching, amoebic way it ascended for ten feet or so. There it vacillated, steadying into a more stable sphere. Then, suddenly, something happened to it. It did not exactly explode. Nor was there any sound. Rather, it seemed to split open, as if it had been burst into instantaneous bloom by a vast number of white cilia which rayed out in all directions.

The instinctive reaction was to jump back from the window away from it. We did.

Four or five of the cilia, like long white whiplashes, flicked in through the window, and dropped to the floor. Almost as they touched it they began to contract and withdraw. Phyllis gave a sharp cry. I looked round at her. Not all of the long cilia had fallen on the floor. One of them had flipped the last six inches of its length on her right forearm. It was already contracting, pulling her arm towards the window. She pulled back. With her other hand she tried to pick the thing off, but her fingers stuck to it as soon as they touched it.

"Mike!" she cried. "Mike!"

The thing was tugging hard, looking tight as a bow-string. She had already been dragged a couple of steps towards the window before I could get after her in a kind of diving tackle. The force of my jump carried her across to the other side of the room. It did not break the thing's hold, but it did move it over so that it no longer had a direct pull through the window, and was forced to drag round a sharp corner. And drag it did. Lying on the floor now, I got the crook of my knee round a bed-leg for better purchase, and hung on for all I was worth. To move Phyllis then it would have had to drag me and the bedstead, too. For a moment I thought it might. Then Phyllis screamed, and suddenly there was no more tension.

I rolled her to one side, out of line of anything else that might come in through the windows. She was in a faint. A patch of skin six inches long had been torn clean away from her right forearm, and more had gone from the fingers of her left hand. The exposed flesh was just beginning to bleed.

Outside in the Square there was a pandemonium of shouting

and screaming. I risked putting my head round the side of the window. The thing that had burst was no longer in the air. It was now a round body no more than a couple of feet in diameter surrounded by a radiation of cilia. It was drawing these back into itself with whatever they had caught, and the effort was keeping it a little off the ground. Some of the people it was pulling in were shouting and struggling, others were like inert bundles of clothes.

I saw poor Muriel Flynn among them. She was lying on her back dragged across the cobbles by a tentacle caught in her red hair. She had been badly hurt by the fall when she was pulled out of her window, and was crying out with terror, too. Leslie dragged almost alongside her, but it looked as if the fall had mercifully broken his neck.

Over on the far side I saw a man rush forward and try to pull a screaming woman away, but when he touched the cilium that held her his hand became fastened to it, too, and they were dragged along together.

As the circle contracted, the white cilia came closer to one another. The struggling people inevitably touched more of them and became more helplessly enmeshed than before. They struggled like flies on a fly-paper. There was a relentless deliberation about it which made it seem horribly as though one watched through the eye of a slow-motion camera.

Then I noticed that another of the misshapen bubbles had wobbled into the air, and drew back hurriedly before it should burst.

Three more cilia whipped in through the window, lay for a moment like white cords on the floor, and began to draw back. When they had vanished across the sill I leaned over to look out the window again. In several places about the Square there were converging knots of people struggling helplessly. The first and nearest had contracted until its victims were bound together into a tight ball out of which a few arms and legs still flailed wildly. Then, as I watched, the whole compact mass tilted over and began to roll away across the Square towards the street by which the sea-tanks had come.

The machines, or whatever the things were, still lay where they had stopped, looking like huge grey slugs, each engaged in pro-ducing several of its disgusting bubbles at different stages.

I dodged back as another was cast off, but this time nothing happened to find our window. I risked leaning out for a moment to pull the casement windows shut, and just got them closed in time. Three or four more lashes smacked against the glass with such force that one of the panes was cracked.

Then I was able to attend to Phyllis. I lifted her on to the bed, and tore a strip off the sheet to bind up her arm.

Outside, the screaming and shouting and uproar was still going on, and among it the sound of a few shots.

When I had bandaged the arm I looked out again. Half a dozen objects, looking now like tight round bales, were rolling over and over on their way to the street that led to the waterfront. I turned back again and tore another strip off the sheet to put round Phyllis's left hand.

While I was doing it I heard a different sound above the hubbub outside. I dropped the cotton strip, and ran back to the window in time to get a glimpse of a plane coming in low. The cannon in the wings started to twinkle, and I threw myself back out of harm's way. There was a dull woomph! of an explosion. Simultaneously the windows blew in, the light went out, bits of something whizzed past, and something else splattered all over the room.

I picked myself up. The outdoor lights down our end of the Square had gone out, too, so that it was difficult to make out much there, but up the other end I could see that one of the sea-tanks had begun to move. It was sliding back by the way it had come.

Discussion

   a. What monsters have men imagined living in the sea?

   b. More than two-thirds of the earth's surface is water. How can man make more use of the sea? (Read *Dolphin Island* by Arthur C. Clarke.)

   c. Most people have a natural dislike for octopuses, squids, sea anemones, and similar creatures. Why? What features of these creatures are used in this story?

Use Your Imagination

   a. Write your own story about things that come "out of the sea".

   b. Write a diary of one of the survivors of a disaster which killed most of the human race.

c. The end of the world and a new start (e.g. the story of Noah) is a favourite theme in science fiction. (Read *The Day of the Triffids* by John Wyndham or *The Scarlet Plague* by Jack London.) Would men return to a primitive caveman-type of existence?

THE YETI

A PRESENT-DAY MONSTER

(One of the aims of the Himalayan Scientific and Mountaineering Expedition led by Sir Edmund Hillary to Nepal in 1960–1, was to search for evidence for or against the existence of the Yeti, or Abominable Snowman, of Nepalese legend.

Earlier expeditions had found huge footprints which they believed may have been made by the Yeti but no European had ever seen one. According to the sherpas, the Yeti is like a huge ape with a human face, human cunning, and a high-pitched whistling call that preys on human beings.

The expedition recorded many accounts from people who claimed they had seen the monsters.)

Twelve years ago a great snow avalanche swept through the village of Beding. A mother and child cowering in their small rock-and-shingle hut were buried alive. And that, the villagers of Beding remember, was the year Yetis were most frequently heard, calling in their strange whistling way, quarrelling through the cold nights, and leaving their footprints in fresh snow every morning.

"I think they were after the corpses of the avalanche victims," the head lama of Beding's small but beautiful monastery told me.

On another occasion, only two winters ago, a couple of Snowmen descended on the monastery at the time of evening prayer. It was already dark and snowing lightly. The creatures snuff-snuffed about the building, at one point threatening to enter through a window. The terrified lamas clashed their ceremonial cymbals with more than devotional fervour and the Yetis went away into the night, "sounding like humans in great pain".

Yet again some years ago a Nepali official visited Beding with a retinue of servants and trappers. Between them they had a vintage gun, and woe to the plentiful musk deer and pheasant

in the area. The time was winter and a light snow fell every evening. As the head lama of Beding tells it, "The party was settling to sleep one night when they were startled awake by the sound of a heavy animal padding around the hut they occupied. Unmistakably it was a Yeti, and suddenly there was its head, large as a bush, with two flaming eyes, at the window. Not one of the party dared move, not even for the gun. We lamas, hearing the din from our monastery—the Yeti was screaming with frustrated rage—began to blow the big copper horns, and eventually the creature took off in noisy alarm."

Discussion

a. After reading as much of the evidence as you can, prepare a report on the existence or otherwise of the Yeti.

b. How would you plan an expedition to prove or disprove the existence of the Yeti? What equipment would you take with you? What proof would you need?

Use Your Imagination

a. You wake up one morning to find a strange being outside your bedroom window. Describe it and how you scared it away. What happens when you tell other people about it?

b. You are out camping when you hear strange noises in the middle of the night. What are your immediate reactions? What happens?

a Landscape
with too few
lovers.

A New Zealand painter's response to his environment. The painter has written on his work: *A landscape with too few lovers*. Discuss.
(A section from the *Northland Panels* (1958) by Colin McCahon)

MAN
AND HIS
ENVIRONMENT

FIRE

Prometheus   **THE GREAT FIRE**

Fire - Makers

The Great Hare's Gift

THE FUTURE

HINDENBURG

BUSHFIRE

Modern Fire

Exploring the Theme

1. Discuss the use of the word *fire* in the following:
   i. We must have more *fire* in the forwards!
   ii. After they have looted the shops, they will *fire* the whole town.
   iii. He was on *fire* with love.
   iv. He was on *fire* with a raging fever.
   v. We sat in front of a roaring *fire* and listened to the rain.

vi. We had to stand and watch the roaring *fire* destroy our home.
2. What forms can fire take? For example, light from the sun and the atomic bomb. Make out your list.
3. Take each form of fire you listed above, and:
    i. Decide what emotions each form arouses in you.
    ii. Write a real or imaginary account of your experiences associated with a form of fire, stressing your own feelings.
    iii. Either compose an abstract drawing (or painting) which conveys your feeling about fire; or work out a mime, perhaps with a group, which illustrates your reaction to different kinds of fire— the rest of the class can try to guess what kind of fire the mime is concerned with.
4. The man-apes of South Africa were using fire more than two million years ago. Suggest the many different uses man has put fire to since that time.
5. Think back over the past. What fires have become part of history? For example, the fire of Rome during which the Emperor Nero is supposed to have played his violin. Select one of these, and write an imaginative eye-witness account of the fire.
6. Why do people always rush to watch a fire?
7. Look at reproductions of paintings of fires, e.g. *The Burning of the House of Commons* by Turner. What aspects of fire does the painter emphasise?

THE MYTH OF PROMETHEUS

A GREEK MYTH

After the Olympians had cleared the earth of monsters and had totally triumphed over the Titans, they decided to put a new race of beings on the earth, a race which would never be able to challenge the power of the gods but would worship them and build temples to their names.

The wise Titan, Prometheus, who had sided with Zeus and the Olympians, was given the job of creating and teaching the new race.

He was instructed to make the new race out of clay in the shape and form of the Immortals themselves. The only difference between the new race and the gods was the fact that the new race was not to be given the sacred gift of fire which gave the gods their great strength and powers.

Prometheus made the god-shapes from clay and water and

Zeus himself, the Father of the Gods, breathed life into the nostrils of the creations. This is how the first men were made.

These early men were little better than animals even though they had been made in the shape of gods. They did not know how to think or talk; nor were they able to use any of the things they saw and felt around them.

But Prometheus, who had the ability to see ahead into the future, worked patiently with the new creations and taught them all the arts and crafts of life. He showed them how to build houses and to make tools; how to plough the earth and to sow corn, how to reap it when it had grown, to thresh out the grains and grind them between flat stones. He showed them how to catch and tame some of the wild animals; the dog to guard the house and help in hunting; the horse to draw the chariot; the ox to pull the plough; the sheep to provide wool; and the goats to yield milk which might be made into cheese. As well as this, Prometheus gave men the power of speech, taught them the names of things, and even how to read and write.

But it was slow work since fire, the greatest of tools, was missing. Without it food had to be eaten raw, and tools could be made only of stone and wood; bread could not be baked and houses could not be warmed in winter.

Prometheus looked up at the sun travelling across the sky in the golden chariot which Helios drove. His knowledge of the future showed him what must surely happen. Then, calling his brother, Epimetheus, he said, "You have helped me so far but now you must live among men and carry on our work on your own. I am going to give fire to mankind. No doubt Zeus will punish me and so you must guard mankind by yourself. Be careful when I am gone and especially beware of any gift from Zeus."

Prometheus took leave of his brother and set out for Olympus, the home of the gods, with a stalk of the fennel plant in his hand. The stalk was as long as a staff and as hard as wood and its hollow stem was filled with a white pith which would burn slowly and steadily like the wick of a candle.

At the foot of Mount Olympus he was met by Athena, the Immortal daughter of Zeus and Goddess of Wisdom, who had always been friendly to Prometheus and interested in his work for mankind. When she knew what he had decided to do, she led him by secret paths to the summit of the mountain.

As the day drew to an end, Helios drove up in his sun chariot, and Prometheus, hiding by the gateway, needed only to stretch out his fennel stalk and touch the golden wheel. Then, the precious spark concealed under his cloak, he hastened down the mountain side and away into the heart of Arcadia where he heaped up a pile of wood and kindled it.

The first people to see the wonderful new gift of fire were the wild satyrs who lived in those lonely valleys. Prometheus was amused at their delight in the warm dancing creature and at the boldest among them who attempted to kiss it and thus burnt his beard.

But he had more serious work in hand, and as soon as day dawned he began to teach men the uses of fire. He showed them how to cook meat and bake bread; how to make bronze and smelt iron; how to hammer the hot metals into swords and ploughshares and all the cunning crafts of the smith and the metal-worker.

Now that fire had come to earth it could be kindled there whenever it was needed. So Prometheus, with the help of Hermes, invented rubbing sticks and taught men which woods to use and how to twirl the hard piece in the soft until fire was kindled by the friction.

When Zeus became aware that his commands had been disobeyed, he summoned Prometheus before him. Prometheus explained why he had given fire to mankind and warned Zeus not to destroy the race of men because in a future day a man would save the gods when their rule was threatened by powerful enemies. A more sinister prophecy Prometheus uttered. Just as Zeus had seized power from his father so in the distant future might Zeus be toppled from his throne.

The anger of Zeus knew no bounds; he ordered Hephaestus to bind Prometheus to the great mountain of the Caucasus on the eastern edge of the world. "There you shall lie," pronounced the Father of the Gods, "for all time, as a punishment for your disobedience. You shall freeze in the winter time and the summer sun will burn you; and your fate will be a warning to all who would disobey."

But Zeus was troubled by the warning of Prometheus and he sent Hermes, the messenger of the gods, to find out all that Prometheus knew of the future. Despite an offer of friendship, Prometheus refused to disclose any of his knowledge. Zeus sent every kind of torture to make his prisoner reveal his secrets but to no avail. Finally he resorted to the cruellest torture of all: an eagle was sent to Prometheus every day to devour his liver; every night, however, the liver grew again and the next day the agony was repeated.

For thousands of years the sufferings of Prometheus continued, a reminder to men of how much they owed their first teacher and a clear sign of the terrible power of mighty Zeus. Finally in a later age the hero Hercules killed the eagle and released Prometheus from his chains when he needed the wise Titan's advice. Prometheus then revealed his long-kept secret to Zeus who forgave him but ordered the rebel to wear an iron band on his finger as a reminder of his punishment. This is why men first wore rings on their fingers.

Discussion and Research

a. Could you prove that the Prometheus story is a myth and not fact?

b. How does the Christian idea of God and creation differ from the picture of the Greek Gods given here? Are there any similarities?

c. *Those who serve mankind nearly always suffer.* Consider the lives of some famous men and women who have contributed to our civilisation. Do their lives prove or disprove the quotation above? (E.g. explorers, nurses, musicians, scientists, politicians, inventors.)

d. Should man stop trying to challenge the gods? Would it be better for him to just worship and build temples as Zeus intended?

e. Why have men set such value on discovering what will happen in the future? Find out what you can about the famous astrologer, Nostradamus, and his prophecies.

Use Your Imagination

a. You are Prometheus on the rock. Tell something of your experiences.

b. Your explanation for the Wearing of Rings.

c. How The First . . . Discovered Fire.

d. Life on Earth Without Fire.

e. Look at the painting *Prometheus* by Titian. What aspects of the myth stimulated the painter?

THE GREAT HARE'S GIFT

A CANADIAN INDIAN MYTH

Glooscap the Great Hare is the hero-magician of the Algonquin Indians of North America. He is called the Great Hare because he has the power of changing himself into that animal. The Indians never cease to tell stories of his strength and wisdom and particularly of his trickery.

In the days when Glooscap was young the people had no fire to warm themselves or to cook their food. Because they saw its destructive power when lightning set the forest ablaze, they were greatly afraid of it.

Eventually fire was brought back from the underworld but its use was forbidden and it was kept as a holy thing on an island where it was well guarded by the chief magician and his two daughters.

As Glooscap himself was young and strong, the lack of fire did not greatly trouble him. But his grandmother, Nokomis, who had brought him up, was growing old and she felt the cold severely. One day in the depth of winter when Nokomis was huddled in her fur cloak trying to keep warm, Glooscap tried to cheer her up by suggesting a hunt in the forest.

The old woman answered him, "It is all very well for a young man like you to speak of the hunting trail; but I am old and slow and the bitter wind bites into my old bones."

Glooscap began to understand the suffering of old age and he was filled with pity. At that moment he began to plan a way to steal fire to be her comfort in the next winter.

In the months before the next winter he set out in his canoe for the region where the sacred fire was kept. His canoe took him across the lake and to the island on which the magician lived. Hiding his canoe in trees on the edge of the island, he changed himself into a Great Hare. Then he jumped into the water to make himself look very wet and bedraggled, for he was sure that this would arouse the pity of the magician's daughters.

As soon as he approached the house where the fire was kept one of the girls saw him and picked him up and carried him into the house, placing him near the burning brand to warm and dry him. Then she returned to her work.

As soon as he was sure no one was watching him, Glooscap

hopped closer to the fire. His sudden movement, however, woke the old magician himself who had been sleeping on a heap of furs in the corner.

The old man's suspicions were aroused and he asked what foolish tricks they had been up to while he was asleep. He caught sight of the hare and got up to have a closer look at the animal. The trembling creature seemed so helpless that he merely remarked on the foolish whims of girls and went back to sleep.

Glooscap waited until he could hear the snores of the old man and until the girls were working as far away from the door as possible. Then, he changed himself back into a fleet-footed Indian brave, seized one of the brands, and dashed out of the house towards his canoe.

The magician was awake at once and he realised immediately who the Great Hare had been. His cries sent the girls in hot pursuit. They knew what would be in store for them if they let the fire be stolen.

Glooscap was confident of his ability to outrun two girls but when he glanced back over his shoulder he was dismayed to see that they were gaining on him every second. Their magic powers helped them to run faster than the wind.

Realising that they would reach him before he could gain his canoe, . . .

Discussion

    a. Old people always seem to complain about the thoughtlessness of young people. What sort of allowances do you have to make for elderly people and why?

    b. What is magic, e.g. of witches, sorcerers? Why were they so important to ancient people?

Use Your Imagination

Write an ending to this myth. You can compare yours with the original by turning to page 161.

THE FIREMAKERS

AN AUSTRALIAN ABORIGINAL MYTH

One day long ago in the time before the tribes learnt to make fire, Bootoolga, the crane, was idly rubbing two sticks together when he happened to notice a slight puff of smoke. He rubbed the sticks harder and again he saw the smoke.

"Look what happens when I rub these two pieces of wood together," he said to his wife Goonur, the kangaroo rat. This time they both saw the puff of smoke.

"Wouldn't it be good if we could make fire to cook our food instead of having to leave it in the sun to dry?" said Bootoolga again.

Goonur looked again and after a pause she said, "Split your stick, Bootoolga, and put some grass in the opening. Then even a tiny spark may set it alight."

Bootoolga saw the wisdom of her words and did what she had suggested. After a great deal of rubbing a small flame came from the opening. Just as Goonur had said it would, the spark lit the grass and the stick smouldered and smoked. And so the art of fire-making had been discovered.

"We will keep this secret from all the tribes," Bootoolga said. "When we make a fire to cook our fish, we will go into the bingawingal scrub so no one will see us. We can hide our fire-sticks in the open-mouthed seeds of the bingawingals; but we must carry one with us, hidden in our kumbi."

Bootoolga and Goonur cooked the next fish they caught and found it tasted much better than dried fish. When they came back to camp, they brought some of their cooked fish with them. Some of the members of the tribe, however, noticed that it looked quite different to the usual sun-dried fish and so they asked:

"What did you do to your fish?"

"Let it lie in the sun," was the reply.

Everyone knew that that was not true, and, as the two returned on succeeding days with their food looking quite different, the tribe made up its mind to watch them. Bulooral, the night owl, and Ooya, the parrot, were appointed to follow the two the next time they went off on their own. Therefore, the next day, when Bootoolga and Goonur started off into the scrub with their share of the food, Bulooral and Ooya followed them.

They saw the couple disappear into the scrub but there they lost sight of them. Discovering a high tree just on the edge of the patch of scrub, the trackers climbed up it and from there they saw all that was to be seen. They saw the fire-makers throw down their load of fish, open their kumbi and take a stick from it. The stick, after it had been blown on, was laid under a heap

of leaves and twigs and in no time at all larger sticks were being added to a little fire. Then as the flames died down, they saw the two place their fish in the ashes that remained from the burnt sticks.

Bulooral and Ooya hurried back to camp with their news. After a long discussion everyone agreed on a plan to get possession of the kumbi. It was decided that they would hold a corroboree. The scheme was to get the firemakers so intent on the dancing that they would leave the kumbi unguarded. Biaga, the hawk, would pretend to be sick and would lie down near Bootoolga and Goonur to watch the proceedings. As soon as they were completely engrossed he would steal the kumbi with the fire-stick in it.

All the tribes were invited and the Brolgas were asked particularly because their famous dancing was most likely to hold the attention of the firemakers. When the day arrived every tribe turned up in its brightest colours ready for the occasion. No one present could remember so many people and such variety of body painting and design.

As Bootoolga and Goonur sat down in the place of assembly, Bootoolga warned his wife not to take an active part in the corroboree and to guard the kumbi carefully. Goonur slung it over her arm but it was not long before she forgot it and in the excitement of the moment let it slip from her arm. But before Biaga could seize it, Bootoolga noticed it and warned his wife again.

Goonur took more care after that but with the dancing of the Brolgas came the chance that Biaga had been waiting for. Everyone was carried away by the humour of their antics and as Goonur joined in the applause she threw herself back helpless with laughter. The kumbi slipped from her arm and immediately the sick Biaga jumped up, snatched the kumbi, cut it open with his knife, and set the grass alight with the fire-stick—all this before the two had realised their loss.

Bootoolga and Goonur tried to catch the thief but they soon realised that with the burning grass beside them, it was useless to try and guard their secret any more. It had now become the common property of all the tribes assembled there.

Discussion and Research

a. Could this myth be based on fact? Why is this myth more

likely to be based on fact than the myths of Prometheus or Glooscap?

b. Is there any significance in the parts played by the male and the female in this story?

c. Should scientists of one country share their discoveries with scientists of another country? Should one country keep discoveries to itself? Does this myth suggest an answer to these questions?

Use Your Imagination

a. Draw, paint, or mime the main scenes in this myth, especially the corroboree. You should have fun working out the dance movements which have to be *antics* to make Goonur *helpless with laughter!*

b. The Day I was Selfish—And What Happened.

c. How to Steal A . . .

THE GREAT FIRE OF LONDON

FROM *PEPYS' DIARY*

Sept. 2nd (1666). Lord's day. Some of our maids sitting up late last night to get things ready against our feast today, Jane called us up about three in the morning, to tell us of a great fire they saw in the City (London). So I rose, and slipped on my night-gown, and went to her window; and thought it to be on the backside of Marke Lane at the farthest, but being unused to such fires as followed, I thought it far enough off; and so went to bed again and to sleep.

About seven rose again to dress myself, and there looked out at the window, and saw the fire not so much as it was, and further off. So to my closet to set things to rights after yesterday's cleaning. By and by Jane comes and tells me that about 300 houses have been burned down tonight by the fire we saw, and that it is now burning down all Fish Street, by London Bridge. So I made myself ready presently, and walked to the Tower; and there got up upon one of the high places; and there I did see the houses at that end of the bridge all on fire, and an infinite great fire on this and the other side the end of the bridge. So down, with my heart full of trouble, to the Lieutenant of the

Tower, who tells me that it began this morning in the King's baker's house in Pudding Lane, and that it hath burned down St Magnus's Church and most part of Fish Street already. So I down to the water-side, and there got a boat, and through bridge, and there saw a lamentable fire. Poor Mitchell's house, as far as the Old Swan, already burned that way, and the fire running further, that, in a very little time it got as far as the Steele-yard, while I was there. Everybody endeavouring to remove their goods, and flinging into the river, or bringing them into lighters that lay off; poor people staying in their houses as long as till the very fire touched them, and then running into boats, or clambering from one pair of stairs, by the water-side, to another. And, among other things the poor pigeons, I perceive, were loth to leave their houses, but hovered about the windows and balconys, till they burned their wings and fell down.

Having stayed, and in an hour's time seen the fire rage every way; and nobody, to my sight, endeavouring to quench it, but to remove their goods, and leave all to the fire; and having seen it get as far as the Steele-yard, and the wind mighty high, and driving it into the City; and everything after so long a drought, proving combustible, even the very stones of the churches; I to White Hall, with a gentleman with me; and there to the King's closet in the Chapel, where people come about me, and I did give them an account that dismayed them all, and word was carried in to the King.

So I was called for, and did tell the King and the Duke of York what I saw; and that, unless his Majesty did command houses to be pulled down, nothing could stop the fire. They seemed much troubled, and the King commanded me to go to my Lord Mayor from him, and command him to spare no houses, but to pull down before the fire every way. The Duke of York bid me tell him, that if he would have any more soldiers, he shall.

Here meeting with Captain Cocke, I in his coach, which he lent me, to Paul's; and there walked along Watling Street, as well as I could, every creature coming away loaden with goods to save, and, here and there, sick people carried away in beds. Extraordinary good goods carried in carts and on backs.

At last met my Lord Mayor in Canning Street, like a man spent, with a handkerchief about his neck. To the King's message, he cried, like a fainting woman, "Lord! what can I do? I am spent; people will not obey me; I have been pulling down houses, but the fire overtakes us faster than we can do it." That he needed no more soldiers; and that, for himself, he must go and refresh himself, having been up all night.

So he left me, and I him, and walked home; seeing people all distracted, and no manner of means used to quench the fire. The houses, too, so very thick thereabouts, and full of matter for burning, as pitch and tar in Thames Street, and warehouses of oil, and wines and brandy, and other things.

Having seen as much as I could now, I away to White Hall by appointment, and there walked to St James's Park; and there met my wife, and Creed, and walked to my boat; and there upon the water again, and to the fire up and down, it still increasing and the wind great. So near the fire as we could for smoke; and all over the Thames, with one's faces in the wind, you were almost buried with a shower of fire-drops. This is very true; so as the houses were burned by these drops and flakes of fire, three or four, nay, five or six houses one from another. When we could endure no more upon the water, we to a little alehouse on the Bankside, and there stayed till it was dark almost, and saw the fire grow; and, as it grew darker, appeared more and more; and in corners and upon steeples, and between churches and houses, as far as we could see up the hill of the City, in a most horrid, malicious, bloody flame, not like the fine flame of an ordinary fire. We stayed till, it being darkish, we saw the fire as only one entire arch of fire from this to the other side of the bridge, and in a bow up the hill for an arch of above a mile long; it made me weep to see it. The churches, houses and all on fire, and flaming at once; and a horrid noise the flames made, and the cracking of houses at their ruin. So home with a sad heart, and find everybody discoursing and lamenting the fire.

Sept. 3rd. About four o'clock in the morning, my Lady Batten sent me a cart to carry away all my money, and plate, and best things, to Sir W. Ryder's at Bednall Greene, which I did, riding myself in my night-gown in the cart; and Lord! to see how the streets and the highways are crowded with people running and riding, and getting of carts at any rate to fetch away things. I find Sir W. Ryder tired with being up all night and receiving things from several friends.

Sept. 4th. Up by break of day to get away the remainder of my things which I did by lighter. To Tower Street, and there

met the fire burning, the fire coming on in that narrow street on both sides with infinite fury. Sir W. Batten not knowing how to remove his wine, did dig a pit in the garden, and laid it in there; and I took the opportunity of laying all the papers of my office that I could not otherwise dispose of. And in the evening Sir W. Penn and I did dig another and put our wine in it; and I my parmazan cheese and some other things. . . .

Walking into the garden, saw how horribly the sky looks, all on afire in the night, was enough to put us out of our wits; and, indeed, it was extremely dreadful, for it looks just as if it was at us, and the whole heaven on fire. I after supper walked in the dark down to Tower Street, and there saw it all on fire. Now begins the practice of blowing up of houses in Tower Street, those next the Tower, which at first did frighten people more than anything; but it stopped the fire where it was done, it bringing down the houses to the ground in the same places they stood, and then it was easy to quench what little fire was in it. Paul's is burned and all Cheapside.

Sept. 5th. About two in the morning my wife calls me up, and tells me of new cries of fire, it being come to the bottom of our lane. I up and resolved to take her away, and did, and took my gold, which was about £2,350, down by boat to Woolwich; but Lord! what a sad sight it was by moonlight, to see the whole City almost on fire, that you might see it as plain at Woolwich, as if you were by it. So back again, by the way seeing my goods well in the lighters at Deptford, and watched well by people. Home, and whereas I expected to see our house on fire, it being now about seven o'clock, it was not. But going to the fire, I find by the blowing up of houses, and the great help given by the workmen out of the King's yards sent up by Sir W. Penn, there is a good stop given to it, as well as at Marke Lane end as ours. I up to the top of Barking steeple, and there saw the saddest sight of desolation that I ever saw; everywhere great fires, oil cellars, and brimstone, and other things burning. I became afraid to stay there long, and therefore down again as fast as I could, the fire being spread as far as I could see.

Discussion

    a. What is the origin of the word *panic*? Why do people panic?

    b. Should the authorities be allowed to pull down houses to prevent a fire spreading? Should they be allowed to pull

down your house to put through a new motorway?
  c. What would you take with you if you had to evacuate your home in a hurry?
  d. Find out what facts you can about the Great Fire of London. Look on a map of London and see how much of the city was burnt.
  e. Your city or town has been almost destroyed by fire. What improvements would you like to see in the newly-built city? Draw up plans for a well-designed city or town.

Use Your Imagination
  a. Your city, or nearest large town, is on fire. Write a diary covering the three days of the fire.
  b. Write the arguments of one of the householders who refused to let the Lord Mayor pull down his house to prevent the fire spreading.
  c. Write a story based on a situation where people panic.

BUSHFIRE

FROM *ASH ROAD*

(Peter Fairhall is looking for his grandmother in a small Australian town threatened by a huge bushfire. Almost all the other people have been evacuated.)

He ran, not blindly but with difficulty, into the face of fierce heat, expecting his Gran to appear, wraithlike, out of the smoke. She didn't. He drew nearer and nearer to the tempestuous crest of the long hill, the blind crest that marked so distinctly the division between the little world where the Fairhalls and the Buckinghams and the others lived, and the beginning of the great world beyond. But still she did not appear.

He came to the crest, and a spectacle of outrageous splendour stormed and funnelled and sheeted. The fire was a mile away, perhaps only half a mile, he did not know; except that the dam had not stopped it, that in the midst of it the dam bubbled and steamed unseen, and the Robertson's blew up unseen, and the Collins', shrivelled into the earth.

It came upon his vision as something living and evil, shapeless

and formless, constantly changing, huge beyond comprehension: an insane creature of immense greed consuming everything around it whether the taste pleased it or revolted it, rejecting what it did not care for only after it had mauled and savaged it, then pitching it aside or spitting it into the heavens. The heavens shrieked with the indigestible things that the fire hurled from its mouth, spraying after them a froth of fury, flaying them with its ten thousand tongues, whipping before it the terror-stricken survivors of the deep green forest: screaming rabbits and wallabies, bush rats and mice, milch goats and cows, dogs and cats, children's ponies and wombats as fat as pigs, lizards and snakes, and creeping and crawling things. But not Gran Fairhall.

Peter ran on as if drunk, pushed by the fierce winds that now roared not over or through the monstrous thing that filled the valley, but towards it; winds sucked in from cooler places that fed smoke and dust and debris in gigantic clouds, in gigantic whorls, back into the furnace; winds that deflected the searing heat of the advancing furnace, and deflected smoke and vapours and dust and rubbish straight up to the sky. Cool air and boiling air met thunderously, explosively, and ahead of it Peter found his Gran at the roadside.

Though she had fallen heavily she felt no pain. She was past feeling, past caring; mercifully dazed and stupefied.

"I'm here, Gran," Peter called.

She gave no response.

"Gran! You must get up!"

She didn't move.

"Gran," he roared, "Get up!"

She looked at him vaguely as if confronted by a stranger, and deliberately, positively, he slapped her face. He shocked himself, for the impact stung through his hand and through his head. It sharpened her and it sharpened him. "Get up," he screamed.

And she got up, heaving her bulk onto her feet, tottering, until he slapped her again. "Move," he screamed. "Move yourself," and grabbed her arm and dragged, and she came after him like a reluctant beast yoked to a heavy load.

He fought off the road, through the ditch, heaving and pulling her into the sharp scrub, the scrub like needles—the acacias, the sword grass, the dogwood, the brambles, the burrs—and tumbled her through the wire fence into the potato paddock. She collapsed into a heap again, limp and quivering, and he slapped her back on to her feet with ferocious determination, screaming at her, "You will not die. You will not." He propelled her across the face of the hill, across the line of the furrows, driving her like a broken-down bullock, until a huge blast of incredible heat seared out of the north across the open ground. He had an instant's warning, a reflex, and threw her down with paroxysm of strength, and dropped beside her, and the blast went over him like raw fire.

If Peter had still been a boy of only thirteen years, he would have cried then from the pain through his thin singlet and from the bitter, bitter disappointment. They were going to die here; they were never going to rise again because the abhorrent thing raging and writhing across the valley was upon them. But he didn't cry, didn't have time to cry, because suddenly, blasting back out of the south, came cooler winds: winds still of great heat, but cooler, roaring back in again with dust and debris in stinging clouds.

He found his feet again, almost blinded. The face of the hill was still there, like an ocean rock swept by spume, or a desert prominence lashed by sand, or metal liquifying in a crucible. The face of the hill was there but it was no longer motionless, no longer immovable. It seemed to slip and slide, shivering like an agitated fluid, heaving. It would not remain fixed, and Peter dropped again, felled by the heat and sound and dizziness.

It wasn't the hill; it was in his head, in his body, in his blood.

He got up again, and his grandmother rose like a drugged creature of low intelligence responding to unwanted orders, and together they moved again, wading rather than running, as if the earth had turned to mud and sought to hold them fast; on, as in a dream, across the curiously contoured brow of the hill with the heavens above them like a breaking wave: a breaker of blackness and brilliance and satanic grandeur, of scarlet and gold and purple, blue and orange, brown and black, turbulence and oiliness and gas: a breaker perpetually at the point of breaking, curved, crested, like a flare from the face of the sun.

Peter fell and the earth fell with him, shot from under his feet. He skidded and tumbled, rolled in a shower of dirt and pebbles, over and over, steeply down the face of the rocky subsidence; his Gran somewhere near him, rolling and tumbling through grass and burns and scrub, her cries unheard, her hurts unfelt.

They tumbled into the pool among the basalt boulders, into

the welling spring that was the source of the creek below Grandpa Tanner's and the Buckingham's.

The water was shockingly cold.

With them in the water were creatures of the forest, things that crept and crawled, even snakes.

But there was a new sound in the heavens, a sighing, as if a giant as large as the earth had expelled the last breath from its lungs. Every living and growing thing bent to it, shuddering as it passed. And then there was a light of another kind, and sound of another kind, and in the sky a collision, a convulsion, a conflict of giants.

Peter saw it, for it happened above him, to his left and his right, all around him, a flash of incredibly brilliant light from sky to earth or earth to sky, and an explosion that stunned him, numbed him, almost crushed him.

Then it fell like huge hot drops of metal, heavy like the sap of trees or globules of honey. It was even the colour of honey, sometimes burnt honey, sometimes golden.

The juices of the forest so greedily sucked up, the heavy juices of gum and pine and acacia, and the blood of beasts and the steam of ditches and ponds and creeks and rivers and reservoirs, of tanks and hoses, of irrigated fields and mud puddles, seemed to have weakened, having allowed the first drops to fall, they seemed to be spilling the lot over.

Black rain, red rain, golden rain, steaming rain, crashed onto the earth, and the sound was real thunder and the jagged light was real lightning and the giants of north wind and south wind, of the inferno and of the breath of the wide cool sea, were locked in conflict.

Peter and Gran Fairhall dragged themselves from the spring, away from the snakes and the other swimming creatures, and the mammoth flare in the sky had dissolved, had vanished, had become a tempestuous brown fog.

Gran, confused but revived, awfully battered but conscious, wrapped her huge fleshy arms about her grandson, as she was often apt to do, and hugged him tight. For years Peter had detested it, had endured it with a set face and a pounding heart; but that had been the way of a boy, not the way of a man. Gran even sensed the difference herself and faintly heard his voice: "It's all right, Gran. Everything's all right now."

Discussion

   a. Why do some people reach a stage when they completely give up? Why did Peter slap his grandmother's face and what effect did it have?

   b. Peter feels that he has now become a man after his rescue of his grandmother. Why should he feel like this? What makes a person grow up?

   c. Try and explain, scientifically, why a huge bushfire can sometimes cause a rain storm similar to that which saved the people of Ash Road.

Use Your Imagination

   a. Write a story of the rescue of someone who does not want to be rescued.

   b. Write an account of fighting a fire, basing it on your own experience if possible.

   c. Find out what you can about the life of a fire watcher in the forest service. Write a story based on this situation.

THE *HINDENBURG* DISASTER

A NEWS COMMENTARY

(In 1937, the airship *Hindenburg* crossed the Atlantic in less than forty-eight hours. American radio commentator, Herb Morrison, is describing it coming in over the mooring-post at Lakehurst, New Jersey.)

   . . . It's practically standing still now. The ropes have been dropped and they've been taken hold of by a number of men on the field. It is starting to rain again. The rain had slacked up a little bit. The back motors of the ship are just holding it . . . ah, just enough to keep it from . . .

   It's burst into flame! Get out of the way; get out of the way! Get this started; get this started. It's on fire and it's crashing. It's crashing terrible! Oh my! Get out of the way, please!

   It's burning, bursting into flames and it's falling on the mooring-pads and all the folks there! This is terrible! This is one of the worst catastrophes in the world! Oh . . .Oh! The flames are twenty . . . are four or five hundred feet into the sky.

   It's a terrific crash, ladies and gentlemen. It's smoke and it's flames now and the frame is crashing to the ground, not quite to the mooring-mast. All the humanity! All the passengers! I don't believe . . . I can't even talk . . . people whose friends are all there. I can't talk, ladies and gentlemen!

Honest it's a mass of smoking wreckage! Ladies . . . I'm sorry. I can hardly . . . I am going to step inside where I can't see it. This is terrible! Listen, folks, I'm going to have to stop for a minute because I've lost my voice.

Discussion and Research

   a. Find out as much as you can about Fire Insurance. How much does it cost to insure your home? Does it make any difference what your house is made of? How much would you get if your house was totally destroyed by fire?
   b. Discuss the effectiveness of your school's fire-fighting equipment and fire drill.

Use Your Imagination

You are a radio or TV commentator. You are covering one of the following events when something unexpected happens:
   a. A race at an evening meeting of the local trotting club.
   b. A concert in your local hall (or town hall).
   c. Arrival of important overseas visitors at the airport.
   d. The visit of an official to a factory.

OUR MODERN FIRE

I. FROM *HIROSHIMA*

The two men set out. The morning was perfectly clear and so warm that the day promised to be uncomfortable. A few minutes after they started, the air-raid siren went off—a minute-long blast that warned of approaching planes but indicated to the people of Hiroshima only a slight degree of danger, since it sounded every morning when an American weather plane came over. The two men pulled and pushed the handcart through the city streets. . . . As they started up a valley away from the tight-ranked houses, the all-clear sounded. (The Japanese radar-operators, detecting only three planes, supposed that they comprised a reconnaissance.)

Pushing the handcart up to the rayon man's house was tiring, and the men, after they had manoeuvred their load into the driveway and to the front steps, paused to rest a while.

Then a tremendous flash of light cut across the sky. Mr Tanimoto has a distinct recollection that it travelled from east to west, from the city toward the hills. It seemed a sheet of sun. Both he and Mr Matsuo reacted in terror—and both had time to react (for they were 3,500 yards, or two miles, from the centre of the explosion). Mr Matsuo dashed up the front steps into the house and dived among the bedrolls and buried himself there. Mr Tanimoto took four or five steps and threw himself between two big rocks in the garden. He bellied up hard against one of them. As his face was against the stone, he did not see what happened. He felt a sudden pressure, and then splinters and pieces of board and fragments of tile fell on him. He heard no roar. (Almost no one in Hiroshima recalls hearing any noise of the bomb.)

When he dared, Mr Tanimoto raised his head and saw that the rayon man's house had collapsed. He thought a bomb had fallen directly on it. Such clouds of dust had risen that there was a sort of twilight around. In panic, not thinking for the moment of Mr Matsuo under the ruins, he dashed out into the street. He noticed as he ran that the concrete wall of the estate had fallen over—towards the house rather than away from it. In the street, the first thing he saw was a squad of soldiers who had been burrowing into the hillside opposite, making one of the thousands of dugouts in which the Japanese apparently intended to resist invasion, hill by hill, life for life; the soldiers were coming out of the hole, where they should have been safe, and blood was running from their heads, chests, and backs. They were silent and dazed.

Under what seemed to be a local dust cloud, the day grew darker and darker.

He thought of a hillock in the rayon man's garden from which he could get a view of the whole of Hiroshima and he ran back up to the estate.

From the mound, Mr Tanimoto saw an astonishing panorama. Not just a patch of the suburb, as he expected, but as much of Hiroshima as he could see through the clouded air was giving off a thick, dreadful miasma. Clumps of smoke, near and far, had begun to push up through the general dust. He wondered how such extensive damage could have been dealt out of the silent sky; even a few planes, far up, would have been audible. Houses nearby were burning, and when huge drops of water the size of marbles began to fall, he half thought that they must be coming from the hoses of firemen fighting the blazes.

Mr Tanimoto found about twenty men and women on the sandspit. He drove the boat on to the bank and urged them to get aboard. They did not move and he realised that they were too weak to lift themselves. He reached down and took a woman by the hands, but her skin slipped off in huge, glove-like pieces. He was so sickened by this that he had to sit down for a moment. Then he got out into the water and, though a small man, lifted several of the men and women, who were naked, into his boat. Their backs and breasts were clammy, and he remembered uneasily what the great burns he had seen during the day had been like: yellow at first, then red and swollen, with the skin sloughed off, and finally, in the evening, suppurated and smelly. With the tide risen, his bamboo pole was now too short and he had to paddle most of the way across with it. On the other side, at a higher spit, he lifted the slimy living bodies out and carried them up the slope away from the tide. He had to keep consciously repeating to himself, "These are human beings." It took him three trips to get them all across the river. When he had finished, he decided he had to have a rest, and he went back to the park.

The morning again was hot. Father Kleinsorge went to fetch water for the wounded in a bottle and a teapot he had borrowed. He had heard that it was possible to get fresh tap-water outside Asano Park. Going through the rock gardens, he had to climb over and crawl under the trunks of fallen pine-trees; he found he was weak. At a beautiful moon bridge, he passed a naked, living woman who seemed to have been burned from head to toe and was red all over. Near the entrance to the park, an Army doctor was working, but the only medicine he had was iodine, which he painted over cuts, bruises, slimy burns, everything—and by now everything that he painted had pus on it. Outside the gate of the park, Father Kleinsorge found a tap that still worked—part of the plumbing of a vanished house—and he filled his vessels and returned. When he had given the wounded the water, he made a second trip. This time the woman by the bridge was dead. On his way back with the water, he got lost on a detour around a fallen tree, and, as he looked for his way through the woods, he heard a voice ask from the underbush, "Have you anything to drink?" He saw a uniform. Thinking there was just one soldier, he approached with the water. When he had penetrated the bushes, he saw there were about twenty men, and they were all in exactly the same nightmarish state: their faces were wholly burned, their eye-sockets were hollow, the fluid from their melted eyes had run down their cheeks. (They must have had their faces upturned when the bomb went off; perhaps they were anti-aircraft personnel.) Their mouths were mere swollen, pus-covered wounds, which they could not bear to stretch enough to admit the spout of the teapot. So Father Kleinsorge got a large piece of grass and drew out the stem so as to make a straw, and gave them all water to drink that way. One of them said, "I can't see anything." Father Kleinsorge answered, as cheerfully as he could, "There's a doctor at the entrance to the park. He's busy now, but he'll come soon and fix your eyes I hope."

•   •   •   •   •

Statistical workers gathered what figures they could on the effects of the bomb. They reported that 78,150 people had been killed, 13,983 were missing, and 37,425 had been injured. No one in the city government pretended that these figures were accurate —though the Americans accepted them as official—and as the months went by and more and more hundreds of corpses were dug up from the ruins, and as the number of unclaimed urns of ashes at the Zempoji Temple in Koi rose into the thousands, the statisticians began to say that at least a hundred thousand people had lost their lives in the bombing. Since many people died of a combination of causes, it was impossible to figure how many were killed by each cause but the statisticians calculated that about twenty-five per cent had died of direct burns from the bomb, about fifty per cent from other injuries and about twenty per cent as a result of radiation effects. The statisticians' figures on property damage were more reliable: sixty-two thousand out of ninety thousand buildings destroyed, and six thousand more damaged beyond repair. In the heart of the city, they found only five modern buildings that could be used again without major repairs.

It would be impossible to say what horrors were embedded in the minds of the children who lived through the day of the bombing of Hiroshima. On the surface, their recollections, months after the disaster, were of an exhilarating adventure. Toshio Nakamura, who was ten at the time of the bombing, was soon able to talk freely, even gaily, about the experience, and a few weeks before the anniversary he wrote the following matter-of-fact essay for his teacher at Nobori-cho Primary School: "The day before the bomb, I went for a swim. In the morning, I was eating peanuts. I saw a light. I was knocked to little sister's sleeping place. When we were saved, I could only see as far as the tram. My mother and I started to pack things. The neighbours were walking around burned and bleeding. Hataya-san told me to run away with her. I said I wanted to wait for my mother. We went to the park. A whirlwind came. At night a gas tank burned and I saw the reflection in the river. We stayed in the park one night. Next day I went to Taiko Bridge and met my girlfriends Kikuki and Murakami. They were looking for their mothers. But Kikuki's mother was wounded and Murakami's mother, alas, was dead."

II. A SCIENTIST'S VIEW

Man has always relied on the sun. Its energy is essential for the growth of living things and it is the driving force behind the weather. The fuels and the electricity so essential for our present standard of living obtain their energy indirectly from the sun. Coal and oil have formed from the remains of plants and small animals which have grown under the sun and dams for hydro-electricity are filled by rain water which comes from water evaporated by the sun.

Where does the sun obtain the energy it radiates as heat and light? It cannot come from burning ordinary fuels as we know them, as these would be exhausted in a very short time. Since the sun has been burning for many millions of years, there must be some other source of energy responsible. If man knew what this was and could duplicate it on the earth, he would have a source of energy to last him almost indefinitely instead of running out as coal and oil eventually will. Many of man's wildest dreams would be within grasp: our living standards could be shared with all men; space travel would become a certainty, to mention merely two.

It was not until the beginning of this century that man began to learn of the origin of the energy of the sun. It was found that the nuclei of some atoms, for example uranium and radium, would spontaneously disintegrate into lighter nuclei at the same time giving off a tremendous quantity of energy. In other words, matter itself could be converted directly into energy. Here was a mechanism which could account for the sun's enormous energy.

There was, however, a danger in these *nuclear* disintegrations. They were radioactive, that is they emitted high energy particles and rays which could damage living tissue, and even cause death. But, surprisingly, it was this particular property of these nuclear disintegrations which was first used for man's benefit. By the controlled use of radioactivity it is possible to destroy unwanted growths, such as tumours and cancer, in the human body. Today radioactivity is widely used in medicine, scientific research and industry.

Although harmful radioactivity could be turned to man's advantage with care, it did not give him a practical source of energy. The outbreak of World War II provided the incentive for man to make an attempt to use this source of energy—to produce a super-bomb of terrific explosive force. Most of the world's greatest physicists were gathered together in the United States and the expenditure of two billion dollars, and three years work by 150,000 workers were required before the atomic bomb became a reality. After the war the large body of knowledge gained in producing the bomb was turned to the building of nuclear power stations and, more recently, nuclear-powered ships.

Nuclear power stations provide a valuable source of power but they do not yet use the nuclear reaction going on in the sun. This has been used, though, in the hydrogen bomb. In this reaction lighter nuclei are combined together to form heavier ones and it is in this way that the sun converts matter to energy. The so-called H-bomb is many times more powerful than the ordinary atomic bomb and can be made as powerful as man wants, giving us the ultimate in destructive forces. As yet the problems of producing the necessary high temperatures to start the reaction under controlled conditions has not been overcome.

(The H-bomb uses an ordinary atomic bomb to do this.) Until this can be done, and much more research is needed, man cannot claim that he can control the source of the sun's energy and use it for mankind's benefit.

Discussion and Research

a. In what ways is the discovery of atomic energy similar to the discovery of fire by primitive man?

b. If your capital city were destroyed by an atomic bomb, what effects would this have on the rest of the country? Write a story which shows some of the after-effects in action.

c. Nuclear physicists have warned of the dangers of atomic warfare. Who is to blame if they are not listened to?

d. Is the use of the atomic bomb any different to the use of any other new weapon, e.g. bow and arrow?

e. What are the dangers of a nuclear war? Read a Civil Defence bulletin. What is the best thing to do in the event of a nuclear attack on your city or a nearby city?

f. Are wars necessary for man's scientific advance?

Use Your Imagination

a. Describe a city in the year 2500 AD to show how man has learned to control and use atomic power.

b. Imagine you were a member of the crew of the B.29 that dropped the bomb on Hiroshima. Write an account of your mission.

c. Imagine what life would be like tomorrow if all the oil and coal ran out overnight.

d. Listen to the 4th Movement of *Symphony No. 6* by Vaughan Williams, which is said to be inspired by the destructive power of the atomic bomb.

THE GREAT HARE'S GIFT (ending)

Glooscap plunged the burning stick into the grass over which he was running. "Here is your fire!" he shouted. The dry grass caught fire immediately and the wind carried the flames and smoke towards the girls, who were forced to stop.

As Glooscap watched the blaze he had made, he saw the

colours of the fire reflected in the broad-leafed trees. The brilliant shades of red, gold and bronze so pleased him that he decided to make them look this way every year.

Glooscap then fixed the burning brand in one end of his canoe and paddled swiftly back to his own country. He soon reached home, and Nokomis received the gift joyfully, basking in the warmth it gave her.

The people soon lost their fear and never tired of telling how the great Glooscap brought them fire.

FLOOD

Deucalion's Flood

Flood Warning

The Fighters of the Flood

Noah's Ark

RESCUE

Exploring the Theme

1. Discuss the use of the word *flood* in the following:
   i. She burst into a *flood* of tears.
   ii. The Monkees received a *flood* of fanmail.
   iii. The market was *flooded* with butter from other countries.
   iv. The river was in *flood*.
   v. The *flood* cut all communications with the outside world.
2. Research. Consult reference books to prepare a general essay on floods. Consider the causes of floods and the good or bad after-effects.
3. Listen to a record of Dukas' *The Sorcerer's Apprentice*. Prepare a mime of the story in which the apprentice causes a flood.

Twentieth-century man used his imagination to build Noah's Ark for the Twentieth Century-Fox film, *The Bible*.

NOAH AND THE ARK

FROM THE BIBLE

In the days after Adam and Eve had learnt the meaning of evil and suffering, their descendants spread over the face of the earth. But then, as now, the good men who followed the laws of God were greatly outnumbered by those who lived a life of evil. Gradually the wickedness which the original disobedience had brought into the world became so widespread that goodness seemed to be completely conquered by it. It was such a world of greed and lust and deceit that made God decide to destroy mankind and with him all the living things that he had created.

Before he carried out his intentions, however, God examined closely the lives of men and women. Among all the thousands and thousands of descendants of Adam and Eve he found no one whose life was worth saving—no one, that is, except an old carpenter called Noah. Alone, this simple, hard-working man retained an unshakeable belief in goodness and in the God which had made him and the world. This faith helped him to live a life of honesty and kindness which was very different to the life which went on around him.

It was the goodness of this old man and his family that made God change his mind. Mankind would have a new beginning; all would be destroyed, but Noah and his family would survive to give mankind a second chance of proving themselves worthy of God's love.

Immediately God told Noah that he would destroy all mankind. Noah must build an ark, a huge boat able to float on the sea, and large enough to contain Noah, his family and two of every kind of living creature. God had determined to bring a flood to the earth which would cover the surface long enough to wash it clean.

Noah began his task of building the ark amidst the laughter of all his neighbours and friends. Although Noah did his best to warn these foolish people of the coming catastrophe, they did nothing but pour scorn on the busy builder. Aided by his three sons, Shem, Ham and Japheth, the old man worked steadily until at last the huge boat was complete in every detail. The seams were caulked with pitch and stores sufficient for the longest voyage were taken on board. It was, however, the zoo collection of a male and female specimen of every living creature that caused the greatest amusement among the onlookers. Even his own family began to question Noah's sanity; but resolutely he saw to the housing of the huge menagerie.

All the animals had no sooner been shut in their cages than it began to rain. Even then people refused to listen to the crazy old man who persisted in believing that the end of the world was coming. But the rain did not stop and when the river broke its banks and flooded both town and countryside, Noah, his wife and three sons with their wives were safe inside the ark.

Even then the rain did not cease; and when the ark began to float, those on board fully realised the truth of mankind's fate. Soon all the familiar landmarks had disappeared below the surface of the waters and at last the very tops of the hills were submerged. Forty days and forty nights the rain continued to fall and the ark continued to float on an endless ocean of swirling water. For six whole months the waters covered the face of the earth and it was only Noah's sure faith in God's word that enabled the inhabitants of the ark, the only living creatures who remained, to keep alive their hope of once again setting foot on dry land.

At length God sent a drying wind and for another long four months they watched the waters subsiding until they could see the tops of the hills standing firm above the ocean. Noah hopefully released first a raven and then a dove but neither could find a resting-place. Noah waited another seven days before releasing a second dove. This time when it returned to its home, they were able to celebrate, for in its beak was a freshly-plucked, green olive leaf. The end of the long ordeal was in sight. Life had begun again.

Seven days later Noah released the dove again; it did not return. Soon afterwards the ark came to rest on one of the hilltops. Before he set all the living creatures free again, Noah built an altar and worshipped the God who had protected him and who had given mankind a second chance.

This action of Noah's pleased God who determined never again to bring such a flood to the earth. As a sign God set the rainbow in the sky to show that he still watched over the lives of all the descendants of Noah.

Discussion and Research

  a. What was the *original disobedience*?

  b. If God told you that only your family would be saved, what would you put on your *ark*?

  c. What *evils* in the world today do you detest most? Would you include *greed, lust and deceit*?

  d. If God looked around the world today, whose lives might he save?

  e. Is there any significance in the fact that archaeologists have found evidence that there was a great flood, and that a wooden ark, built to the specifications in Genesis, would work?

Use Your Imagination

  a. Write a short story about a modern person who thought the end of the world was coming on a particular day, at a particular time.

  b. Imagine you are on the ark when the waters begin to rise. Write a short play based on conflicts between those on the ark as to what they should do.

  c. The world has been destroyed. Imagine the survivors beginning again.

  d. Write your own myth to account for the rainbow.

  e. Read the miracle play *Noah's Flood* or listen to Benjamin Britten's opera *Noye's Fludde*, based on the play. What changes to the myth have been made? How does the music add to the enjoyment?

DEUCALION'S FLOOD

A GREEK MYTH

Not long after Pandora brought suffering and evil to men so many reports of mankind's wickednesses were brought to Zeus that the Father of the Gods determined to see for himself the way people were living. He called to Hermes to accompany him, saying:

"We will take the form of men and travel among them as poor travellers. If they do not treat us kindly according to the laws of hospitality, I will destroy the whole race of them."

Hermes, who secretly loved mankind and had supported

Prometheus in his work of education, begged his father not to be over hasty. "Mighty Zeus," he said, "if we visit three households and find that two out of three treat us inhospitably, then let mankind be destroyed. But if we find goodness and kindness in even two, no matter how wicked the third one is, spare the good and let the wicked perish."

Zeus agreed to this test and the two Immortals began their wanderings among the people of Arcadia in Greece, Zeus disguised as an old man and Hermes as his son.

The two went first to the palace of King Lycaon, a fierce and evil man who was hated and feared by all the ordinary people in his kingdom. He had fifty sons who were as bad as he was, and like him, cannibals. To begin with the travellers were refused entry but thinking that Hermes would make a good feast, Lycaon bad-temperedly bade them enter and sit at his table. When he learnt that there was no fresh meat in the house, the king ordered that one of his sons, Nyctimus, who had always refused to eat flesh, be killed and put in the pot.

Zeus knew what the dish was as soon as it was placed on the table. Filled with rage, Zeus turned Lycaon and his sons into a pack of howling wolves and sent them away into the forests. Nyctimus was restored to life and set to rule over the country in the place of his father.

"You see," said Zeus, "is there any need to look further? Men are just as bad as I've been told." But Hermes reminded his father of his promise to visit three families and they sought out the hospitality of a poor man. They stopped at the little clay cottage of an old man and his wife whose names were Philemon and Baucis. Poor though the old couple were, they welcomed their guests and did all that was in their power to entertain them. Zeus was pleased and, revealing his true identity to them, asked what they most desired. The couple merely begged to serve the gods in any way possible and to die at the same moment, seeing that they had lived all their lives together.

Zeus changed their mud hut into a magnificent marble temple and appointed the old couple as priest and priestess. At the same time they became young again and thus able to live their lives a second time. Zeus also granted their other request, saying that at the moment of death the two would be turned into trees so that they could stand in the same place and bow their heads before his temple.

The third and final visit the gods made was to the home of Deucalion, King of Thessaly, who had married Pyrrha, the daughter of Epimetheus and Pandora. Fortunately for mankind they found that a king could be as pious and as kindly as the old peasants, for Deucalion treated his guests with great hospitality.

"Now," said the Father of the Gods, "I will return to Olympus and let loose a great flood over the earth. All those who are not fit to live shall be drowned in the flood, and any who are worthy of life shall be led to the tops of the mountains. As for you, Deucalion, you will build a ship large enough to hold your whole family, food and clothing. You will be safe inside the ship and I will guide it to the land over which I desire you and your children to rule."

Deucalion did exactly as the god had commanded, using all the skill that Prometheus had taught him. Soon the ship was finished, and as soon as he and Pyrrha were safely inside, Zeus let loose the rain. For nine days and nights the rain poured down on the earth; and Poseidon, the brother of Zeus and God of the Seas, stirred up the waves with his trident so that the sea flowed in over the land.

All was desolation: houses lay in ruins beneath the waters, the corn turned black and rotted, and the fish swam in and out of the branches of the trees. Only the sea-peoples, the dolphins, were happy, swimming about the mountain tops and diving down to explore drowned cities beneath the waves.

At last the waves began to fall and the ship came gently to rest on the slopes of Mount Parnassus near Delphi. Praising the gods for their deliverance, Deucalion and Pyrrha stepped on to dry land and lay down to sleep.

During their sleep a voice spoke to them from out of the depths of the earth: "Deucalion and Pyrrha, Father Zeus does not mean to utterly wipe out the race of men. Therefore, go down into the valley before you, cover your heads with your cloaks and cast behind you the bones of your mother!"

The two were greatly puzzled by this command when they awoke. Each of them had a different mother, both of whom were dead. At last, however, Deucalion hit upon the right answer. Their real mother was the earth because it was out of the earth that Prometheus had formed the first men. The bones of their mother, earth, must surely be the stones.

At once they went down into the river valley, covered their heads and began to throw stones backwards over their shoulders. Soon they could hear a murmuring noise behind them. As they continued to throw the stones, the noise continued to grow. Finally they could restrain themselves no longer and when they turned round, there in front of them was a huge crowd of men and women. They could see the last few stones they had thrown swell and change, grow soft and rise up as human shapes. Men came from the stones which Deucalion had thrown and women from those thrown by Pyrrha.

In this way the land of Greece was repeopled, and very soon new cities sprang up from the ruins of the old; the fields produced rich corn once more and the olive groves shimmered silver in the sunlight.

The children of Deucalion and Pyrrha, with the few who had survived the flood by climbing to the mountain-tops, became the kings and queens of the various states of Greece.

Discussion and Research

a. What differences are there between this myth and the story of Noah?

b. Do you think that poor people are more virtuous than rich ones?

c. Was Zeus fair? (Begin by considering the test.)

d. Use reference books to find out about sunken cities (e.g. Atlantis) and legends of sea monsters, mermaids, and other underwater curiosities.

e. If a complete stranger came knocking at your door asking for a meal, would you invite him in? Try and account for the change in the laws of hospitality since the days of the Greeks.

Use Your Imagination

a. Describe your discovery of an underwater town, or your exploration of an underwater wreck.

b. Write a poem with two stanzas: one describing the scene before a flood, the other after a flood.

THE FIGHTERS OF THE FLOOD

A CHINESE MYTH

The Yellow Emperor, Ruler of Heaven, had for a long time been grieved at the way men on earth were living in wickedness. Finally his sorrow turned to anger and he decided that a terrible punishment would be the only way to make men forsake their evil way of life. The punishment he chose for his task was rain— the endless, torrential rain which brings the flood. Kung-Kung, the cruel Spirit of Water was placed in charge because the Emperor knew that he would carry out his duties without mercy.

When the rain began the people were forced to leave their fields to find shelter inside. Everyone knew these rains: paths would soon be impassable, the hollows would fill with water and the small streams would flood the fields. But this time the rains did not stop. Anything that had been left outside was soon soaked through and rotted. Holes appeared in the thatch roofs of huts and people began to feel desperate for food and shelter.

Many of these suffering human beings were suddenly caught in a swirling mass of water. The river had broken its banks! Some of them were able to reach the hills and others sought safety in the top branches of tall trees. But most were drowned in the angry, yellow waters. For those who escaped drowning there was no food save the leaves and bark of the trees and the only water, the flood itself.

Fortunately for mankind there was one spirit who had watched from above this terrible scene of suffering and destruction and was moved to pity by it. This was Kun, the grandson of the Emperor. Kun went to the Ruler of Heaven and begged him to show mercy, but he was unable to shake the determination of his grandfather.

Sadly he left the Emperor's throne and confided his problem to his friends the horned owl and the black tortoise. Together they hatched a desperate and daring plot to steal the Magic Mould with which the Ruler of Heaven had made the earth. Even a little portion of the Mould would grow into any size its possessor required. Kun knew that this was the only hope for mankind and he was prepared to risk the anger of the Emperor.

No one ever found out exactly what their plan was or how they were able to gain a piece of the jealously-guarded Mould. The important thing was that their plan worked and Kun with a tiny lump of the precious Mould descended to the earth and began his fight against the flood. On the top of a high mountain overlooking a vast sheet of water covering what had once been a heavily-populated valley, Kun broke off the smallest piece of Mould that he could and threw it into the water. He ordered it to grow until he told it to stop, and then he stood back and waited. He was just beginning to think that it would not work when his sharp eyes noticed a slight movement in the water. A few moments later it seemed as though the land was rising, and then in different places soil broke through the surface of the water. What had been a deep lake was now only a swamp. The Mould kept on growing until all the water had been absorbed and when finally the valley was filled with rich, brown soil, Kun ordered it to stop.

Kun watched only long enough to see a dazed handful of men stumble out of their caves to touch the new earth that had been given to them so miraculously. He turned to other areas for there was no time to lose before the Emperor found out what he had done and ordered his death. Unwearyingly he travelled up and down the country filling up the valleys and raising the plains. Everywhere he dropped a speck of the precious Mould the flood waters were soaked up like a sponge. Kun did more than this; across the plains he built channels to drain off the water which was still falling; and along the river he built high stop-banks to keep the river in its own bed.

Before Kun could complete his task, however, the theft of the Magic Mould and the work that Kun had done with it were reported to the Yellow Emperor. There could be only one punishment for such disobedience and treachery in Heaven. That was death! The Emperor immediately dispatched the Spirit of Fire with the task of executing Kun and recovering the Magic Mould.

The Spirit of Fire was too powerful for Kun and although he tried to escape, he was caught by the Spirit on the Feather Mountain near the North Pole and there executed. His body was left on the mountain in the cold and dark where the only light comes from the candle in the mouth of the Candle Dragon which guards those desolate wastes.

But it is not a simple matter to kill a heavenly being and although the physical body of Kun lay lifeless, the force of the compassion which had led him to commit the crime preserved his body from decay. Inside the body a change was occurring; a new being, Kun's son, was in the process of creation. The work of Kun must be continued because there were still areas deep under water and already many of the fields created by Kun were beginning to sink again beneath the water.

After three years had passed the Emperor received a report that the body of Kun had undergone no change. Fearing a rebirth of the traitor, he sent another Spirit to destroy the body. As the Spirit flashed his sword into the body, out flew a horned dragon, which spread its wings and soared into the sky. This was Yu the great, the spirit born of Kun's will to fulfil his task of fighting the floods.

The dragon flew straight to the court of the Yellow Emperor who granted him an audience. Yu spoke to the Emperor in true submissiveness and begged him to consider whether the miserable people on earth had not suffered enough to learn the lesson of their past wickedness. The Emperor was still angry about the theft of the Magic Mould but the strength and youthful determination of Yu appealed to him.

The Ruler of Heaven reflected and then granted Yu's request. He was permitted to have as much of the Magic Mould as could be piled on the back of the old tortoise who had helped Kun before. Yu's father was also granted a pardon and his form was changed into that of a dragon like his son.

Yu collected the Mould, and, assuming human form, returned to the earth. His first task was to control the cruel Kung-Kung who was still delighting in his work of punishing mankind. Together with his friend the Stormguard, Kung-Kung refused to listen to the Emperor's command to end the rains and storms. Yu was forced to act sternly and with right on his side he executed the Stormguard on Mount Hui-chi as a warning to all those who disobey the Yellow Emperor. Many hundreds of years later men found a bone of the body of the Stormguard on Mt Hui-chi, a bone so big that it took twenty men to lift it into a cart. The other rebel, Kung-Kung, fled from Yu and no one has ever learnt of his hiding-place.

Now Yu could carry out his main task. Like his father before him, he filled up the valleys, drained the plains, built banks to keep the river within its course. For many years he laboured and his efforts drew the gratitude of all mankind. Yu, his work complete, was made Emperor on earth. When he died, a very

old man, his body was buried on Mount Hui-chi but his spirit returned to Heaven to live forever.

Discussion

a. What facts did the Chinese want to explain by this myth?
b. What makes this myth different from the story of Noah?
c. Compare the Chinese, Greek, and Jewish ideas of *God*.
d. Was Kun right in disobeying the Yellow Emperor? Are there any times when it is right to break laws and disobey those in authority? Are there any laws which may never be broken?
e. Try to explain why the flood story appears so widely in different mythologies, e.g. Australian Aborigines, Mexicans, Goths.

Use Your Imagination

a. Using a Chinese style of painting (consult reference books for examples), paint a scene from this myth.
b. Assume that there is a heaven. Describe it.
c. You have been given some of this Magic Mould. What would you do with it? Write a story about your actions.
d. Write another explanation of the huge bone found on Mount Hui-chi.

FLOOD WARNING

FROM A FRENCH STORY

(The boys and masters of Chateau-Milon school in southwestern France have been cut off from the rest of the world by the serious flooding of the Loire and its tributaries. The school is surrounded by six-feet-high stone walls and the water is rapidly rising around these walls. Everyone has worked feverishly to build a sand-bag dam to block the gap where the gate in the walls usually was. Vignoles, a senior pupil, and Monsieur Sala, a junior master, are on watch during the early morning hours. The water has begun to trickle over the top of the walls and is stretched out in a huge lake around them. The master has just reported to the headmaster.)

Monsieur Sala hurried off towards the garden. He splashed

through the puddles which bubbled in the rain. Vignoles had not left his ladder (which lent against the wall). He leaned right over the parapet, literally hypnotised by the sight of the slumbering flood whose weight he could almost feel stirring against his body.

"Come down! Hurry! Let's get out of here!" Monsieur Sala shouted, wild with alarm.

Away to their left, there was a dull crash and then the drumming of the rain was drowned by a roaring which increased in volume and came from behind the trees. Vignoles reached the ground and shook his dripping waterproof. The noise had become so loud that they could hardly hear themselves speak.

"Wait for me by the corner of the hard courts," he shouted to Monsieur Sala. "I'm going to see what's happened."

He was off at once, holding his torch over his head. Thirty yards farther on he suddenly found the flood up to his knees. The water boiled over the fallen trees and swept through the shrubberies.

Vignoles struggled foot by foot against the current.

The beam of his torch swept from side to side, then suddenly focused. The boy stopped, his heart in his mouth. At the far end of the garden ten or fifteen feet of wall had caved in. Through the gap thundered a solid stream of swirling ice-grey water.

In the background Monsieur Sala's voice sounded feebly.

"Come back, Vignoles! Come back at once! We'll both be caught!"

Vignoles retraced his steps, fighting his way like a madman through the broken branches tangled across his path. In several places the water was flooding over the top of the wall and bringing whole sections of it crashing down. As far as the eye could see the garden was under two feet of water.

Vignoles jumped for the hard courts. They were deserted.

"Where are you?"

As he turned he saw the flicker of Monsieur Sala's torch by the dam as he ran, his own pointed in that direction. Suddenly he could see the little man spreadeagled across the sandbags, trying with his feeble strength to restrain an ocean. At the same time Vignoles could see the sinister shiver as the whole mass of the dam almost imperceptibly began to topple backwards.

"Have you gone mad?" he shouted. "Get away!"

Furiously he tugged at Monsieur Sala's shoulders. They both

fled for their lives. Thirty yards lay between them and the hard courts and then there were the steps to climb. Their feet were on the first of these when there was a crash that made the earth tremble and a stream of water came jetting from the gate and caught them between the shoulder blades. Vignoles heaved and hauled his companion to the plateau of the courts. They turned and switched on their torches.

The sandbag dam had given in one solid mass, opening the gardens to the flood. Directly before them and almost at their level a turbulent river flowed noisily in and spread out among the trees. In a few minutes the gate-posts were gone like melting snow under the tremendous pressure. Then there was a sinister crack as the whole wall shuddered and fell in a lump that broke to right and left as the water drove through.

In an instantaneous flash Monsieur Sala and Vignoles saw the wave hang ten feet high. They fled for the headmaster's house as fast as their legs could carry them. All round them the darkness was a confusion of gurgling, crashing, hissing water like the noise of the waves on a shelving beach. The flood gathered on the ground it had won, to sweep on to fresh conquests.

Use Your Imagination

    a. You are a student at a small country school. The school is caught in a flash flood. Write a story about this.

    b. Write a story or play about a family isolated in a farmhouse by rising floodwaters. The main conflict would be whether someone should go for help or not. Try to show the different reactions to danger by different personalities in the family.

    c. Imagine you are one of the boys at the Chateau-Milon school. Write an account of how you were rescued from the flood. (In the story a helicopter is used to rescue some of the boys.)

RESCUE

FROM *ICE COLD RIVER*

(A river in North Canterbury, New Zealand, has flooded, marooning people in their farmhouses. In one house is a young teenage boy, Hugh, who has a boat. When this story begins he has just launched it to take an eighteen-year-old girl back to her own house.)

At last he managed to steer from the current and make the high knoll, where cows and sheep were clustered, feeding casually. And Sheila's heart bumped, because immediately she thought that her father might be there, and would help them. Hugh jumped out to prevent *Waltz* grounding hard, and they lifted her to safety, out of the slapping water, and Sheila ran about, calling "Dad! Dad! Are you here?" but nobody answered, and the place seemed more desolate, suddenly, and the evening darker.

Hugh was shipping the mast, and called her to help him.

"Why are you doing that?" she asked.

"To sail her."

"Back against the wind?"

"What else?"

Sheila remembered the boats on the lower reaches of the river, sails taut, flattening almost into the water, then riding into the gusts with the canvas like iron, till at last the tension eased and the sails grew limp. Sometimes they cracked, then, like pistol shots.

Hugh bent his head, fastening the forestay. He had been brusque, rude, since they left the house. He was hurt and angry. Perhaps, too, thought Sheila, he was frightened. As she was, herself.

But she was older. Therefore she must help him, not become flustered.

"We can try, anyway," she said. "You must tell me what to do."

"I shan't set the jib. All you'll have to do is to stay where I tell you. And hike when I tell you."

"Hike?"

"Lean out. If she heels too far."

Sheila looked dubious.

"We must try," said Hugh. "We can't stay here all night."

"No," agreed Sheila, again dubiously.

"It's a pity I didn't have the sail set at first. We would have made your house on a broad lead. Now we must beat."

Sheila tried to look intelligent. She did not understand a word. But she hoped that if they were tipped out it would happen soon, so that they could reach dry land without much difficulty. They lifted *Waltz* carefully into the water, and Sheila stood holding the

bow, while Hugh raised the sail, which threshed and whipped, and seemed, to Sheila, a great deal to handle.

"Hop in!" said Hugh. "Come on, hurry up!"

But though Sheila fell in awkwardly as fast as she was able and Hugh hauled frantically at the mainsheet, the current was so strong that the boat was swept in a wide arc before she began to sail.

"Sit up! Sit up!" shouted Hugh. "Beside me!"

They almost met disaster in those first moments. The sail filled, *Waltz* heeled under the vicious wind, and both—Sheila by pure instinct—threw themselves to windward. Very slowly at first, and then with a jerk, *Waltz* righted herself, and Hugh bore off again, this time with extreme caution. *Waltz* charged across the floodwaters, rushing, then hesitating, surging again precariously.

It was a crazy uneven battle. On the first leg, because of the strong current, they gained no ground, in fact were driven back. In changing course they almost capsized for the second time, and the boat swung in a circle. Now we must swim, thought Sheila despairingly, and wondered how deep the water was. But Hugh managed to gain control, and they staggered half-way back to the knoll before finally *Waltz*, with a slow inevitability that was horrible to share, dipped the sail in the water, half filled, swung upright again, then filled completely from over the stern and sank like a drowning animal, the hull completely submerging before turning over and placing the sail, like a collapsed parachute, in the water.

Sheila noticed that Hugh pulled up the centreplate first. Then he turned to her and said, "Are you all right?" Sheila, clinging grimly to the gunwale, was shaking with cold and with fright, but said, "I suppose so."

"We mustn't drift too far. Hang on and kick. If I can pull her upright I'll get the sail down."

It was borne in on Sheila that what mattered was not themselves, but the boat. Her instinct was to strike out for dry land, but this, she soon saw, was not the thing to do. Hugh would pull his boat ashore if she froze or collapsed in the process.

After a few moments she was able to subdue her panic, and look about her. They were not so far from safety, after all. She tried to touch bottom, but could not. After a good deal of struggling Hugh managed to right the boat, but she turned turtle twice more before he could lower the sail. Then they both moved to the stern, and, kicking, tried to propel the waterlogged *Waltz* to safety.

It was almost impossible to move her across the current towards the high ground. They drifted on an oblique course, so that there grew a real danger of being swept past altogether. What happens then, thought Sheila, panic growing again. Drift into the south branch? Though there are plenty of willow trees there to tie to. But she did not relish the thought of spending the night in a tree.

Surely the flood water petered out somewhere? Spread wide, lost force, pooled in the meadows in a still, soiled lake, redolent yet of disaster, but exhausted now, and spent?

Sheila kicked with all her strength, but the boat seemed very heavy, and she was becoming feeble. The water slapped in her face, and by now she had swallowed a good deal of it. It was very dirty, and tasted horrible. What with that, and fright and exhaustion, she felt sick. We'll never make it, she thought in despair.

They would indeed have been swept on but that Sheila swallowed more water, retched, and in complete anguish put her feet down.

They touched bottom. She stood, hung on to the stern of the boat with all her might, gasped and spluttered.

"What is it?" said Hugh, gasping too.

"Bottom. I can stand."

"Get round to the bow, then. Pull! Go on! What are you waiting for?"

Sheila retched again. She turned her face from Hugh and clawed her way to the bow. Now they were able to make more progress. Soon Hugh was able to find bottom too, and came to the bow to help her.

By the time they lifted *Waltz* clear it was almost completely dark. The sheep were dim white blobs, the cows almost invisible. But Sheila had noticed, during the wretched task of bailing the boat, when they could both scarcely stand, that the level of the flood had risen. They might yet spend the night in a tree, she thought wearily. But she was too tired to think of it much, or to worry about the animals. Her legs were jelly. All she was fit for was to lie still for a little while, quite still.

Use Your Imagination

a. You disobey your parents, or someone in authority, with disastrous or unfortunate consequences. Write your story.
b. Imagine you are drowning. Write a poem about your thoughts.
c. Exploring a river, an underground cave, or part of a lake— write about what you discover.
d. Sheila felt that Hugh cared more for his yacht than for her safety. Write a new version of the story including dialogue in which she accuses him of this.

THE ANIMAL WORLD

Gift of God   *TRAP*

Monkey's Mischief   **Fables**

THE ANT'S NEST

Exploring the Theme

1. How many of the following sayings are, do you think, based on fact?
    i. As wise as an owl?
    ii. As cunning as a fox?
    iii. As cheeky as a monkey?
    iv. As treacherous as a snake?
    v. As busy as a bee?
    How many other sayings give human qualities to animals in this way?
2. Can you produce any evidence that animals can:
    i. think (including reasoning)
    ii. talk
    iii. remember
    iv. understand love and affection
    v. record their experiences.
3. By quoting books, magazines, comics, and television, try to decide which animals are most popular with mankind, and why.
4. What is evolution? Is man an animal or more than an animal? How is he related to the animals?

THE GIFT OF GOD

AN AFRICAN MYTH

In West Africa men tell of the making of all living creatures by the god Aziza who descended from the sky. The animals soon found their rightful places in the land, the monkey in the trees, the buffalo in the swampy areas and the lion in the savannah grassland. Here they lived according to the laws of Aziza.

Then men came. Where they came from or how nobody knows but they were weak-looking creatures who walked upright like apes but carried sharp sticks in their hands. Only they did not obey the laws of Aziza. They trespassed on the elephant's preserves as well as those of the lion. They were too untrustworthy, too forgetful of the laws for any animal to become their friend. And thus there were two worlds of life living alongside each other but never taking the other into consideration, never understanding the other.

But in the two worlds, the world of men and the world of animals, all things were the same. For example, men had certain fields where they drew signs and marks in the ground. They would wait until the jackal walked over these marks and then the sorcerer or fortune-teller would read the future and make prophecies. So in the world of animals, the jackal drew signs in certain areas and waited for men to walk over the ground before he could make predictions and give warnings to the other animals.

For many moons things continued like this. Men used animals and animals used men, but neither understood what the other was thinking or doing. Then, purely by accident, the village sorcerer chose to draw his signs in the same field which was used by the jackal. Men waited and wondered what the animals were waiting for; the animals waited and wondered what the men were waiting for. Finally, when each group got the answer it was waiting for, by a great coincidence, it was the same:

A GIFT OF GOD WILL BE LEFT BY THE BIG STONE

Both men and animals knew which big stone was intended and so by evening a great crowd of men and animals had gathered to wait for the gift of God. When it came it surprised everyone with its clear, red beauty and its long tongue which licked around the hollow stone. Its voice crackled with joy and everyone, animals and men, rushed forward to seize the gift that the gods had given them—fire!

But, because neither world understood the other, there was a savage battle resulting from the desire aroused by this new, beautiful arrival. The animals, however, greatly outnumbered the men and eventually their combined strength forced the men to retreat from the big stone. In triumph they chose the elephant, who had played the biggest part in the animals' victory, to carry the glowing prize away. In the heart of the jungle, one place which man had never reached, they set the red gift on a rock surrounded by water. This would be its home. If the animals had not made the mistake of thinking of the red gift as an animal like themselves, it seems probable that men would never have learnt the use of fire.

The animals felt that they must feed this living red thing or else it would die. They therefore fed it things like coconuts and fruit and soon learned that its favourite food was dry leaves and the dead branches of trees. The red animal continued to grow and wanted more and more to eat. One day, however, while the monkey was taking his turn at feeding the red animal he threw a long piece of liana or creeper around it because he had decided it would like to feed in the jungle, for a change. The red animal immediately ate the liana and climbed along it up into the tree in which the monkey was perched.

It attacked the tree and soon gobbled it up. By now the monkey was very frightened and he turned and fled into the jungle. But the red animal was still tied to the liana and this the monkey still had in his hand. Everything it touched was devoured until the whole jungle seemed to become part of the red animal. The monkey and the other animals tried to flee and suddenly found themselves in the lake where the village of the men was. Here the red animal paused to drink. It drank and drank and the lake was reduced in size but as it swallowed the water, its belly shrank. At last it collapsed like a dying animal leaving heaps of broken red bones. Men came and picked up the red bones and carried them to their village, hiding them under the ashes.

In this way men came to tame the gift of fire which the animals had lost and to make it work under their cooking pots. From that time onwards all animals have avoided the red animal whose nature they never fully understood.

Discussion and Research
  a. Is man born good or bad? Or neither, or both?
  b. What makes people *bad*? Is anyone ever completely bad?
  c. Do you avoid things you don't understand? Give examples.
  d. Is there danger in using things you do not understand or have control over, e.g. a motor car, electricity, alcohol?
  e. In what ways is fire like an animal?
  f. What is a coincidence? Have there ever been any unusual coincidences in your life? Why are they widely used in stories? Discuss coincidences in stories you have read recently.

Use Your Imagination
  a. Write a story which illustrates the superiority of animals over humans.
  b. Write a story about a gift which proved to be more trouble than it was worth.
  c. God gives mankind another gift in the year 2000. What is it? How does man react to it?

THE MONKEY'S MISCHIEF

A WEST INDIAN MYTH

The people of Trinidad in the West Indies tell this story of why man cannot understand the animals.

In the first days of the world man and the animals lived a life of understanding and co-operation. The first men who lived on the terraces of the river on the edge of the dark green jungle did not fear the jaguar nor did the jaguar crouch motionless and tense at the sight of man. Even the wild pig had no fear of the sound of man's feet on the jungle floor.

Most of the animals worked together with man. The parrot, who, as today, sat preening his bright feathers, called out all the news to man as he passed by. The snake often went in front of man and showed him the quickest and easiest paths through the thick jungle. The dog, the baboon and the sloth helped man to do all sorts of jobs although it is true that the sloth frequently fell asleep in the middle of some work.

Roger Hart

In return, man helped all the animals to find food. If he cut down a tree, he would always give the animals pieces of the tree to plant near their homes as well as taking cuttings for his own needs. He knew and did not forget that every animal felt the same thirst and hunger that sometimes pinched him.

There was, however, one animal who never helped in any of the work. This was the restless little brown monkey who was always playing a trick on one of the other animals. He would pinch the wild pig, pull the tail of the wild cow, shake the branch on which the parrot was perched and leap on the back of the jaguar as he lay dozing in the sun. It was this trouble-maker who nearly destroyed man and brought an end to the friendship between man and the other animals.

One day man cut down a great tree and to his surprise a stream of water began to gush from its roots. In reply to man's question the water said that it was flowing so fast in order to cover the face of the earth by the next day.

Man cried out to the Ancient One asking what he could do to prevent such a disaster. He was told that the only way to stop the flow was to make a huge basket of reeds and to cover the hole that the water was gushing out of, with it. Man quickly made the basket and as soon as it was placed over the flowing stream the water ceased.

All would have been well had it not been for the brown monkey who had seen man making the basket. He followed him and from the top of a tall tree he saw the basket being put over the hole. The monkey remembered some of the tricks he himself had played and thought: "Man is hiding the best fruit underneath the basket so he doesn't have to share it with us. I'll take the basket away as soon as he goes off and taste the food."

The monkey did take the basket away and the stream flowed even faster than it had done before. The monkey was swept away in the flood and only his cries were heard by the parrot. When the other animals discovered what was happening, they cried out to man to save them.

Man realised at once the danger and he rushed the animals to the top of the nearest hill. A grove of coconut-trees was growing right on the top of the hill and all the animals were herded to the top of these.

For five days they lived in the green branches at the top of the trees, and for all that time the water kept rising higher and higher. On the second day a mist came down out of the sky and the rain fell in sheets.

Most of the animals were very frightened but the baboon was more terrified than anyone. All that time he kept up his shrill cries until they became hoarse croaks. By the end of the five days his throat had grown to twice its size and his voice had changed from a shrill cry to a deep roar. That is why to this day baboons have the largest throats and the loudest voices in the jungle.

Suddenly on the evening of the fifth day, the rain stopped, the thunder died away and the lightning ceased to flash. In the morning the sun rose but the earth was still covered by the mist so that it was impossible to see the ground. The animals wanted to climb down from the trees but before he let them, Man dropped a coconut and listened. Almost at once there was a splash, and everyone knew that it was no use climbing down yet.

Every day man dropped a coconut and every day the splashing seemed further away and the coconut took longer to hit the water. On the tenth day the coconut made not a splash but a dull thud. Eagerly, the animals began to climb down from their trees, but man ordered them to stay where they were until he had made sure that it was quite safe.

Only the trumpeter bird refused to listen. He was so tired of sitting in the tree that he climbed straight down. Unfortunately, in his hurry, he stepped right into a nest of ants who were coming out of their hiding-place in search of food. Before man could help the trumpeter bird, the ants had stripped the flesh from its long and shapely legs. This is why you will still see the trumpeter bird mourning because his legs are so thin.

The rest of the animals followed man out of the trees, cold, wet and very hungry. Even the wild pig, who so loves a mud bath, tried to find a warm dry place. To cheer the animals, man began to make a fire. He rubbed two sticks together until he kindled enough heat to light his little pile of sticks.

Trouble broke out as soon as man turned his back on the fire. One of the animals, one of the greedy ones obviously, stole the fire for himself. Man was most annoyed because he had to start rubbing two sticks all over again. The alligator who had the longest tongue of all the many animals and who was rather disliked by the others because of his grumpiness, was accused of having swallowed the fire. The alligator was forced to open his mouth to prove his innocence. In his indignation—or it may have been his guilt—he swallowed half his tongue and to this day the alligator has the shortest tongue of all animals.

Who actually stole the fire was never finally discovered. Most of the animals think it was the alligator but some believe a report that it was the marudi bird who had snatched it up the moment that man turned away.

The whole affair caused such an upset that from then onwards man has never trusted the animals and has even lost the ability to speak and understand the same language. Today each animal seems to have its own language: the whistling and chirruping of the birds, the screech of the parrot, the mooing of the cow, the snarl of the jaguar, the hoot of the owl and the grunt of the wild pig. All this because the brown monkey was too fond of playing tricks on people!

Discussion

    a. Do you think discipline is necessary in society (include the family and the school)?

    b. What does the expression *use your initiative* mean?

Use Your Imagination

    a. Explain in a story why certain animals have certain character-istics—e.g. why an elephant has a long trunk; why mice like cheese; or why owls hoot; why the kiwi cannot fly; why the kangaroo carries its babies in a pouch.

    b. Write a story based on a practical joke which misfires.

    c. Write a poem describing an animal in detail. It might be easiest to imagine the animal involved in a particular situation in a particular place.

    d. Listen to a record of the French composer Saint-Saens, called *Carnival of the Animals*. What characteristics of the animals does Saint-Saens illustrate?

FABLES: ANCIENT AND MODERN

Aesop's Fables, supposedly written by a Greek slave of the sixth century, BC, are more probably a compilation of the fables of many writers. (a) Write the moral of each of the five fables of Aesop that follow. (b) Work out a definition of a fable that will fit all the examples in this section.

Write a fable to illustrate the idea that freedom of speech must not be abused, e.g. by slandering others.

The Dog and the Wolf

A very thin and worried-looking wolf once became friends with a well-fed and contented dog. The wolf inquired of his companion how he lived so well.

The dog replied, "Why, I look after my master's house and protect his family from intruders. He gives me all the meat and drink I need and I sleep in a warm comfortable bed. I'm sure if you come along with me I can arrange for you to lead the same kind of happy life."

This pleased the wolf and he said how grateful he would be if such a thing were possible. They were walking in the direction of the dog's home when the wolf suddenly noticed a bare place around his friend's neck. Politely he asked what had caused it.

"Oh, that's nothing," answered the dog, "just the rubbing of my collar a little."

"If that is the case," said the wolf, "I'll be on my way. I know better than to sell my freedom for a full belly." And he returned to his own life.

Discussion
  a. Which do you value most: freedom or security?
  b. Explain the following: freedom of speech; freedom of belief; freedom of the press; freedom of action.

Use Your Imagination
Write a poem in praise of privacy.

The Mouse and the Lion

Once a tiny mouse ran unwittingly over the body of a sleeping lion. The lion awoke and seized the trembling creature. The mouse begged the lion to set her free, promising to repay the lion some day. The lion laughed good-humoredly and let her go.

Not long afterwards the mouse heard the angry roaring of a lion. Being naturally a curious creature she went off to see what the cause of the trouble was. She discovered a lion caught in a net and tied to a tree. She soon found that it was the very same lion that had let her escape earlier.

She said, "You laughed at me the other day because you never expected me to repay your generosity. A mouse is not too small to be able to help a lion sometimes."

And she set to and gnawed through the rope and the threads of the net until the lion was able to escape.

Discussion

Suggest parallels in our world to the Mouse and the Lion, e.g. the Mouse could be a young player and the Lion an experienced sportsman. When they first meet, . . .

Use Your Imagination

Write a story about a very insignificant person who turns out to have surprising resources!

The Eagle and the Crow

A crow sitting in a tree one day noticed an eagle swoop down, seize a lamb in its talons and fly away with it.

The crow was envious and determined to do the same thing. He flew high into the sky and swooped down like the eagle; unfortunately he chose a ram to experiment on. His claws became entangled in the fleece, and he was unable to free himself.

The furious beating of wings and the noise of the sheep attracted the attention of the shepherd, who caught the crow and took him home. He clipped the bird's wings and presented him to his children to play with.

When they asked what sort of bird it was, the shepherd said, "He will try and tell you that he's an eagle but take it from me he's merely an ordinary crow."

Discussion

What is the difference, if any, in the thought behind the following:
a. Know your own limitations.
b. It's not as easy as it looks.
c. Don't bite off more than you can chew.
d. Look before you leap.
e. Don't pretend to be something you are not.

Use Your Imagination

a. Write a poem describing an animal making its kill.
b. Write a description of a person who has a higher opinion of himself than other people think is deserved.

The Wolf and the Lamb

A wolf noticed a lamb grazing on a hillside among a herd of goats. Thinking to entice the lamb down within his easy grasp he said:

"Come down, little one. I will take you back to your mother over in that field."

The lamb bleated, "I am not looking for my mother; my real mother is this goat who nurses me and feeds me."

"Can anyone be dearer to you than the one who gave birth to you?" asked the wolf.

"Why," replied the lamb, "she gave birth to me without knowing or caring what she did; my mother is the one who takes pity on me and cares for me after I am born."

And the wolf went off disappointed.

Discussion and Research

a. Many babies today are legally adopted. Find out about what is involved in this.

b. What was Solomon's Judgement? (Read the play, *The Caucasian Chalk Circle* by Bertolt Brecht.)

c. Do you feel any national, provincial, or civic pride? Is it justified?

Use Your Imagination

a. Write a story to illustrate either of these: cupboard love; blood is thicker than water.

b. Write a description of an ideal mother.

The Lion's Share

A lion, a fox and an ass entered a partnership; they would hunt together, defend one another and live in peace together.

One day after they had been hunting and had caught a number of animals, the lion began to divide their catch into four equal parts. The ass wanted to know why he had divided everything into four parts when there were only the three of them in the partnership.

The lion growled, "The first share is mine as your king; the second is also mine as my share in the hunt. As for the third and fourth portion they are mine unless you care to take them off me."

    a. Do you think you would enjoy living in a society in which everything was shared equally, regardless of your contribution to society?

    b. Do you think things are shared fairly enough in your own society? E.g. everyone has a radio; not everyone has a motor boat.

Use Your Imagination

Write a short story beginning or ending with one of the following:

a. Might is not always right.

b. Possession is only nine-tenths of the law.

A MODERN FABLE

The Tiger Who Would Be King

One morning the tiger woke up in the jungle and told his mate that he was king of beasts.

"Leo, the lion, is king of beasts," she said.

"We need a change," said the tiger. "The creatures are crying for a change."

The tigress listened but she could hear no crying, except that of her cubs.

"I'll be king of beasts by the time the moon rises," said the tiger. "It will be a yellow moon with black stripes, in my honour."

"Oh, sure," said the tigress as she went to look after her young, one of whom, a male, very like his father, had got an imaginary thorn in his paw.

The tiger prowled through the jungle till he came to the lion's den. "Come out," he roared, "and greet the king of beasts! The king is dead, long live the king."

Inside the den, the lioness woke her mate. "The king is here to see you," she said.

"What king?" he inquired, sleepily.

"The king of beasts," she said.

"I am the king of beasts," roared Leo, and he charged out of the den to defend his crown against the pretender.

It was a terrible fight, and it lasted until the setting of the sun. All the animals in the jungle joined in, some taking the side of the tiger and others the side of the lion. Every creature from the aardvark to the zebra took part in the struggle to overthrow the lion or to repulse the tiger, and some did not know which they were fighting for, and some fought for both, and some fought whoever was nearest, and some fought for the sake of fighting.

"What are we fighting for?" someone asked the aardvark.

"The old order," said the aardvark.

"What are we dying for?" someone asked the zebra.

"The new order," said the zebra.

When the moon rose, fevered and gibbous, it shone upon a jungle in which nothing stirred except a macaw and a cockatoo, screaming in horror. All the beasts were dead except the tiger, and his days were numbered and his time was ticking away. He was monarch of all he surveyed, but it didn't seem to mean anything.

Moral: You can't very well be king of beasts if there aren't any.

Discussion and Research

    a. This fable is taken from James Thurber's book *Vintage Thurber*. What is its message for twentieth-century man?

    b. Read Ray Bradbury's short story, *The Flying Machine*. What is its moral?

Use Your Imagination

    a. Write a story with a similar message involving people and countries rather than animals in the jungle.

    b. Write an animal fable to illustrate the idea that it is foolish to judge simply by appearances.

THE ANT'S NEST

FROM *THE ONCE AND FUTURE KING*

(The young King Arthur, known as the Wart, has been locked in his room to recover from a broken collarbone which he received in a fight against a griffin. He is so bored with nothing to do but watch the ant-nests he has collected, that he has begged the magician Merlin, the tutor responsible for his education, to turn him into an ant for a short time.)

The place where he was seemed like a great field of boulders, with a flattened fortress at one end of it—between the glass plate.

The fortress was entered by tunnels in the rock, and, over the entrance to each tunnel, there was a notice which said:

EVERYTHING NOT FORBIDDEN IS COMPULSORY

He read the notice with dislike, though he did not understand its meaning. He thought to himself: I will explore a little, before going in. For some reason the notice made him reluctant to go, making the rough tunnel look sinister.

He waved his antennae carefully, considering the notice, assuring himself of his new senses, planting his feet squarely in the insect world as if to brace himself in it. He cleaned his antennae with his forefeet, frisking and smoothing them so that he looked like a Victorian villain twirling his moustachios. He yawned—for ants do yawn, and stretch themselves too, like human beings. Then he became conscious of something which had been waiting to be noticed—that there was a noise in his head which was articulate. It was either a noise or a complicated smell, and the easiest way to explain it is to say that it was like a wireless broadcast. It came through his antennae.

The music had a monotonous rhythm like a pulse, and the words which went with it were about *June - moon - noon - spoon*, or *Mammy - mammy - mammy - mammy*, or *Ever - never*, or *Blue - true - you*. He liked them at first, especially the ones about *Love - dove - above*, until he found that they did not vary. As soon as they had been finished once, they were begun again. After an hour or two, they began to make him sick inside.

There was a voice in his head also, during the pauses of the music, which seemed to be giving directions. "All two-day-olds will be moved to the West Aisle" it would say, or "Number 210397/WD will report to the soup squad, in replacement of 333105/WD who has fallen off the nest." It was a fruity voice, but it seemed to be somehow impersonal—as if its charm were an accomplishment that had been practised, like a circus trick. It was dead.

The boy, or perhaps we ought to say the ant, walked away from the fortress as soon as he was prepared to walk about. He began exploring the desert of boulders, wandering tracks both aimless and purposeful, which led toward the grain store, and also in various other directions which he could not understand. One of these paths ended at a clod with a natural hollow underneath it.

In the hollow—again with the strange appearance of aimless purpose—he found two dead ants. They were laid there tidily but yet untidily, as if a very tidy person had taken them to the place, but had forgotten the reason when he got there. They were curled up, and did not seem to be either glad or sorry to be dead. They were there, like a couple of chairs.

While he was looking at the corpses, a live ant came down the pathway carrying a third one.

It said: "Hail, Barbarus!"

The boy said "Hail", politely.

In one respect, of which he knew nothing, he was lucky. Merlin had remembered to give him the proper smell for the nest—for if he had smelled of any other nest, they would have killed him at once. If Miss Edith Cavell had been an ant, they would have had to write on her statue: SMELL IS NOT ENOUGH.

The new ant put down the cadaver vaguely and began dragging the other two in various directions. It did not seem to know where to put them. Or rather, it knew that a certain arrangement had to be made, but it could not figure how to make it. It was like a man with a tea-cup in one hand and a sandwich in the other, who wants to light a cigarette with a match. But, where the man would invent the idea of putting down the cup and sandwich—before picking up the cigarette and the match—this ant would have put down the sandwich and picked up the match, then it would have been down with the match and up with the cigarette, then down with the cigarette and up with the sandwich, then down with the cup and up with the cigarette, until finally it had put down the sandwich and picked up the match. It was inclined to rely on a series of accidents to achieve its object. It was patient, and did not think. When it had pulled the three dead ants into several positions, they would fall into line under the clod eventually and that was its duty.

Wart watched the arrangement with a surprise which turned into vexation and then into dislike. He felt like asking why it did not think things out in advance—the annoyed feeling which people have on seeing a job being badly done. Later he began to wish that he could put several other questions, such as "Do you like being a sexton?" or "Are you a slave?" or even "Are you happy?"

The extraordinary thing was that he could not ask these questions. In order to ask them, he would have had to put them

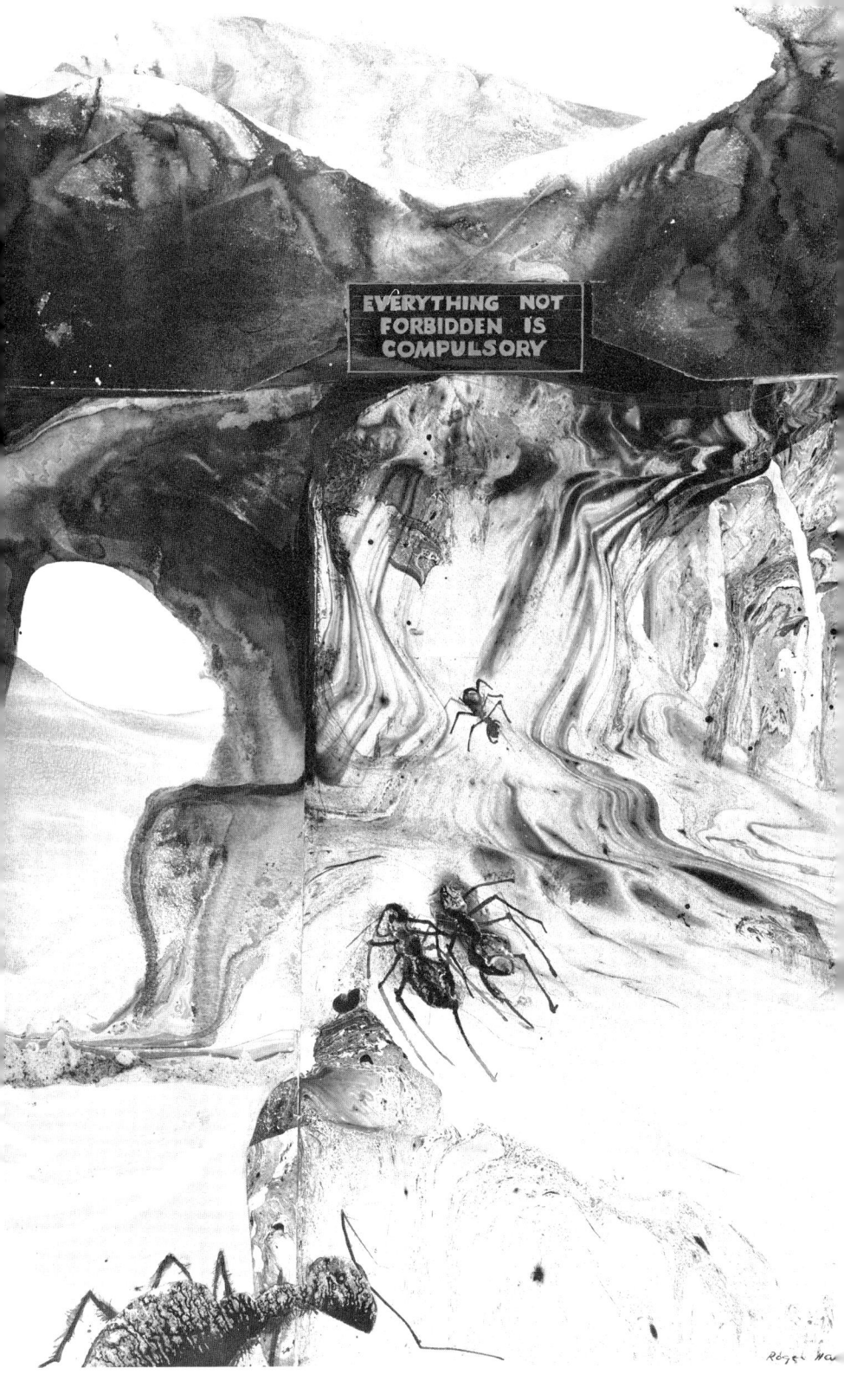

into ant language through his antennae—and he now discovered, with a helpless feeling, that there were no words for happiness, for freedom, for liking, nor were there any words for their opposites. He felt like a dumb man trying to shout "Fire!" The nearest he could get to Right or Wrong, even, was to say *Done* or *Not Done*.

The ant finished fiddling with its corpses and turned back down the pathway, leaving them in the haphazard order. It found that the Wart was in its way, so it stopped, waving its wireless aerials at him as if it were a tank. With its mute, menacing helmet of a face, and its hairiness, and the things like spurs on the front leg-joint, perhaps it was more like a knight-in-armour on an armoured horse: or like a combination of the two, a hairy centaur-in-armour.

It said, "Hail, Barbarus!" again.

"What are you doing?"

The boy answered truthfully: "I am not doing anything."

It was baffled by this for several seconds, as you would be if Einstein had told you his latest ideas about space. Then it extended the twelve joints of its aerial and spoke past him into the blue.

It said: "105978/UDC reporting from square five. There is an insane ant on square five. Over to you."

The word it used for insane was *Not-done*. Later on, the Wart discovered that there were only two qualifications in the language, *Done* and *Not Done*—which were applied to all questions of value. If the seeds which the collectors found were sweet, they were *Done* seeds. If somebody had doctored them with corrosive sublimate, they would have been *Not-Done* seeds, and that was that. Even the moons, mammies, doves, etc., in the broadcasts were completely described when they were stated to be *done* ones.

The broadcast stopped for a moment, and the fruity voice said: "G.H.Q. replying to 105978/UDC. What is its number? Over."

The ant asked: "What is your number?"

"I don't know."

When this news had been exchanged with headquarters, a message came back to ask whether he could give an account of himself. The ant asked him. It used the same words as the broadcaster had used, and in the same voice. This made him feel uncomfortable and angry, two emotions which he disliked.

"Yes," he said sarcastically, for it was obvious that the creature could not detect sarcasm, "I have fallen on my head and can't remember anything about it."

"105978/UDC reporting. Not-Done ant has a blackout from falling off the nest. Over."

"G.H.Q. replying to 105978/UDC. Not-Done ant is number 42435/WD, who fell off the nest this morning while working with mash squad. If it is competent to continue its duties—competent-to-continue-its-duties was easier in the ant speech, for it was simply *Done*, like everything else that was not *Not Done*. But enough of the language question. "If it is competent to continue its duties, instruct 42436/WD to rejoin mash squad, relieving 210021/WD, who was sent to replace it. Over."

The creature repeated the message.

It seemed that he could not have made a better explanation than this one about falling on his head, even if he had meant to—for the ants did occasionally tumble off. They were a species of ant called Messor barbarus.

"Very well."

The sexton paid no further attention to him, but crawled off down the path for another body, or for anything that needed to be scavenged.

The Wart took himself away in the opposite direction, to join the mash squad. He memorised his own number and the number of the unit who had to be relieved.

The mash squad were standing in one of the outer chambers of the fortress like a circle of worshippers. He joined the circle, announcing that 210021/WD was to return to the main nest. Then he began filling himself with the sweet mash like the others. They made it by scraping the seeds which others had collected, chewing up the scrapings till they made a kind of paste or soup, and then swallowing it into their own crops. At first it was delicious to him, so that he ate greedily, but in a few seconds it began to be unsatisfactory. He could not understand why. He chewed and swallowed busily, copying the rest of the squad, but it was like eating a banquet of nothing, or like a dinner-party on the stage. In a way it was like a nightmare, in which you might continue to consume huge masses of putty without being able to stop.

There was a coming and going round the pile of seeds. The ants who had filled their crops to the brim walking back to the inner fortress, to be replaced by a procession of empty ants who were coming from the same direction. There were never any new ants in the procession, only this same dozen going backward and forward, as they would do during all their lives.

He realised suddenly that what he was eating was not going into his stomach. A small proportion of it had penetrated to his private self at the beginning, and now the main mass was being stored in a kind of upper stomach or crop, from which it could be removed. It dawned on him that when he joined the westward stream he would have to disgorge the store, into a larder or something of that sort.

The mash squad conversed with each other while they worked. He thought it was a good sign at first, and listened, to pick up what he could.

"Oh Ark!" one of them would say. "Ear comes that Mammy-mammy-mammy-mammy song again. I dew think that Mammy-mammy-mammy-mammy song is luverly (done). It is so high-class (done)."

Another would remark, "I dew think our beloved Leader is wonderful, don't yew? They sigh she was stung three hundred times in the last war, and was awarded the Ant Cross for Valour."

"How lucky we are to be born in the 'A' nest, don't yew think, and wouldn't it be hawful to be one of those orrid 'B's."

"Wasn't it hawful about 310099/WD! Of course e was hexecuted at once, by special order of ar beloved Leader."

"O Ark! Ear comes that Mammy-mammy-mammy-mammy song again. I do think . . ."

He walked away to the nest with a full gore, leaving them to do the round again. They had no news, no scandal, nothing to talk about. Novelties did not happen to them. Even the remarks about the executions were in a formula, and only varied as to the registration number of the criminal. When they had finished with the *mammy-mammy-mammy-mammy*, they had to go on to the beloved Leader, and then to the filthy Barbarus B and to the latest execution. It went round in a circle. Even the beloveds, wonderfuls, luckies and so on were all *Dones*, and the awfuls were *Not-Dones*.

The boy found himself in the hall of the fortress, where hundreds and hundreds of ants were licking or feeding in the nurseries, carrying grubs to various aisles to get an even temperature, and opening or closing the ventilation passages. In the middle, the

Leader sat complacently, laying eggs, attending to the broad-casts, issuing directions or commanding executions, surrounded by a sea of adulation. (He learned from Merlin later that the method of succession among these Leaders was variable accord-ing to the different kind of ant. In Bothriomyrmex, for instance, the ambitious founder of a New Order would invade a nest of Tapinoma and jump on the back of the older tyrant. There, con-cealed by the smell of her host, she would slowly saw off the latter's head, until she herself had achieved the right of leader-ship.)

There was no larder for his store of mash, after all. When anybody wanted a meal, they would stop him, open his mouth, and feed from it. They did not treat him as a person, and indeed, they were impersonal themselves. He was a dumb-waiter from which dumb-diners fed. Even his stomach was not his own.

But we need not go on about the ants in too much detail—they are not a pleasant subject. It is enough to say that the boy went on living among them, conforming to their habits, watching them so as to understand as much as he could, but unable to ask questions. It was not only that their language had not got the words in which humans are interested—so that it would have been *impossible* to ask them whether they believed in Life, Liberty and the Pursuit of Happiness—but also that it was dangerous to ask questions at all. A question was a sign of insanity to them. Their life was not questionable: it was dictated. He crawled from nest to seeds and back again, exclaimed that the *Mammy* song was loverly, opened his jaws to regurgitate, and tried to understand as well as he could.

Later in the afternoon a scouting ant wandered across the rush bridge which Merlin had commanded him to make. It was an ant of exactly the same species, but it came from the other nest. It was met by one of the scavenging ants and murdered.

The broadcasts changed after this news had been reported—or rather, they changed as soon as it had been discovered by spies that the other nest had a good store of seeds.

Mammy-mammy-mammy gave place to *Antland, Antland Over All,* and the stream of orders were discontinued in favour of lectures about war, patriotism to the economic situation. The fruity voice said that their beloved country was being encircled by a horde of filthy Other-nesters—at which the wireless chorus sang:

'When Other blood spurts from the knife,
Then everything is fine.'

It also explained that Ant the Father had ordained in his wisdom that *Othernest* pismires should always be the slaves of *Thisnest* ones. Their beloved country had only one feeding tray at present—a disgraceful state of affairs which would have to be remedied if the dear race were not to perish. A third statement was that the national property of *Thisnest* was being threatened. Their boundaries were to be violated, their domestic animals, the beetles, were to be kidnapped, and their communal stomach would be starved. The Wart listened to two of these broadcasts carefully so that he would be able to remember them afterwards.

The first one was arranged as follows:

A. We are so numerous that we are starving.
B. Therefore we must encourage still larger families so as to become yet more numerous and starving.
C. When we are so numerous and as starving as all that, obviously, we shall have a right to take other people's stores of seeds. Besides, we shall by then have a numerous and starving army.

It was only after this logical train of thought had been put into practice, and the output of the nurseries trebled—both nests meanwhile getting ample mash for all their needs from Merlin—for it has to be admitted that starving nations never seem to be quite so starving that they cannot afford to have far more expensive armaments than anybody else—it was only then that the second type of lecture was begun.

This is how the second kind went:

A. We are more numerous than they are, therefore we have a right to their mash.
B. They are more numerous than we are, therefore they are wickedly trying to steal our mash.
C. We are a mighty race and have a natural right to subjugate their puny one.
D. They are a mighty race and are unnaturally trying to subjugate our inoffensive one.
E. We must attack them in self-defence.
F. They are attacking us by defending themselves.
G. If we do not attack them today, they will attack us tomorrow.

H. In any case we are not attacking them at all. We are offering them incalculable benefits.

After the second kind of address, the religious services began. These dated—the Wart discovered later—from a fabulous past so ancient that one could scarcely find a date for it—a past in which the emmets had not yet settled down to communism. They came from a time when ants were still like men, and very impressive some of the services were.

A psalm at one of them—beginning, if we allow for the difference of language, with the well-known words, 'The earth is the Sword's and all that therein is, the compass of the bomber and they that bomb therefrom'—ended with the terrific conclusion: 'Blow up your heads, O ye Gates, and be ye blown up, ye Everlasting Doors, that the King of Glory may come in. Who is the King of Glory? Even the Lord of Ghosts, He is the King of Glory.'

A strange feature was that the ordinary ants were not excited by the songs, nor interested by the lectures. They accepted them as matters of course. They were rituals to them, like the *Mammy* songs or the conversations about their Beloved Leader. They did not look at these things as good or bad, exciting, rational or terrible. They did not look at them at all, but accepted them as *Done*.

The time for the war came soon enough. The preparations were in order, the soldiers were drilled to the last ounce, the walls of the nest had patriotic slogans written on them, such as *Stings or Mash?* or *I Vow to Thee, my Smell*, and the Wart was past hoping. The repeating voices in his head, which he could not shut off; the lack of privacy, under which others ate from his stomach while others again sang in his brain; the dreary blank which replaced feeling; the dearth of all but two values; the total monotony more than the wickedness: these had begun to kill the joy of life which belonged to his boyhood.

The horrible armies were on the point of joining battle, to dispute the imaginary boundary between their glass trays when Merlin came to his rescue. He magicked the sickened explorer of animals back to bed, and glad enough he was to be there.

Discussion

    a. How important is work in making a person happy?

    b. What does *you can have too much of a good thing* mean?

    c. In choosing a career, what factors are you going to consider?

What questions are you going to ask about the job? e.g. How much satisfaction will it give me when I am older? Does it offer security? What do other people think of the job?

d. Give examples of snobbery. Are you ever a snob?

e. What examples of propaganda are in this extract? Are you exposed to any propaganda?

f. What is a police state?

g. What were the purposes of the songs which never stopped in the ant's nest? Does music have a similar function for us?

h. Is it right to always ask questions? Are there some things in life which should not be questioned?

i. Find out what you can about brainwashing.

Use Your Imagination

a. Change yourself into an animal, e.g. an eel, a cat, a seagull, a fly. Describe your experiences.

b. Write the lyrics for a propaganda pop song, or a TV singing commercial.

c. Plays like the *Insect Play* and *Donkey in a Thistlefield* and *Toad of Toad Hall* are set in the world of animals. Write a play with song, mime, dance, and dialogue which will involve the whole class. Your setting can be an ant's nest. Your aim is to show that a loss of freedom by the individual is a horrifying prospect.

d. Nightmare!

e. Imagine you are in a society where everything is upside down, e.g. sickness is a crime; and crime is treated as sickness.

TRAP

FROM *SALAR THE SALMON*

(Salar the salmon has just taken the fly.)

A moment later, the fisherman, feeling a weight on the line, lifted the rod-point, and tightened the line, and had hardly thought to himself, salmon, when the blue-grey tail of a fish broke half out of the water and its descending weight bent the rod.

Salar knew of neither fisherman nor rod nor line. He swam

down to the ledge of rock and tried to rub the painful thing in the corner of his mouth against it. But his head was pulled away from the rock. He saw the line, and was fearful of it. He bored down to his lodge at the base of the rock, to get away from the line, while the small brown trout swam behind his tail, curious to know what was happening.

Salar could not reach his lodge. He shook his head violently, and, failing to get free, turned downstream and swam away strongly, pursued by the line and the curious buzzing vibration outside his jaw.

Below the pool, the shallow water jabbled before surging in broken white crests over a succession of rocky ledges. Salar had gone about sixty yards from his lodge, swimming hard against the backward pull of line, when the pull slackened, and he turned head to current, and lay close to a stone, to hide from his enemy.

When the salmon had almost reached the jabble, the fisherman, fearing it would break away in the rough water, had started to run down the bank, pulling line from the reel as he did so. By thus releasing direct pull on the fish, he had turned it. Then, by letting the current drag the line in a loop below it, he made Salar believe that the enemy was behind him. Feeling the small pull of the line from behind, Salar swam up into deeper water, to get away from it. The fisherman was now behind the salmon, in a position to make it tire itself by swimming upstream against the current.

Salar, returning to his lodge, saw it occupied by another fish, which his rush, and the humming line cutting the water, had disturbed from the lie by the sodden log. This was Gralaks the grilse. Again Salar tried to rub the thing against the rock, again the pull, sideways and upwards, was too strong for him. He swam downwards, but could make no progress towards the rock. This terrified him and he turned upwards and swam with all his strength, to shake it from his mouth. He leapt clear of the water and fell back on his side, still shaking his head.

On the top of the leap the fisherman had lowered his rod, lest the fly be torn away as the salmon struck the water.

Unable to get free by leaping, Salar sank down again and settled himself to swim away from the enemy. Drawing the line after him, and beset again by the buzzing vibration, he travelled a hundred yards to the throat of the pool, where water quickened over gravel. He lay in the ripple spreading away from a large stone, making himself heavy, his swim-bladder shrunken, trying to press himself into the gravel which was his first hiding-place in life. The backward pull on his head nearly lifted him into the fast water, for nearly five minutes, until his body ached and he weakened and he found himself being taken sideways by the force of shallow water. He recalled the sunken tree and it became a refuge, and he swam down fast, and the pull ceased to buzz against his jaw. Feeling relief, he swam less fast over his lodge, from which Gralaks sped away, alarmed by the line following Salar.

But before he could reach the tree the weight was pulling him back, and he turned and bored down to the bottom, scattering a drove of little grey shadows which were startled trout. Again the pull was too much for him, and he felt the ache of his body spreading back to his tail. He tried to turn on his side to rub the corner of his mouth on something lying on the bed of the pool— an old cartwheel—again and again, but he could not reach it.

A jackdaw flying silently over the river, paper in beak for nest-lining, saw the dull yellow flashes and flew faster in alarm of them and man with the long curving danger.

Fatigued and aching, Salar turned downstream once more, to swim away with the river, to escape the enemy which seemed so much bigger because he could not close his mouth. As he grew heavier, slower, uncertain, he desired above all to be in the deeps of the sea, to lie on ribbed sand and rest and rest and rest. He came to rough water, and let it take him down, too tired to swim. He bumped into a rock, and was carried by the current around it, on his side, while the gut cast, taughtened by the dragging weight, twanged and jerked his head upstream, and he breathed again, gulping water quickly and irregularly. Still the pull was trying to take him forward, so with a renewal by fear he turned and re-entered fast water and went down and down, until he was in another deep pool at a bend of the river. Here he remembered a hole under the roots of a tree, and tried to hide there, but had not strength enough to reach the refuge of darkness.

Again he felt release, and swam forward slowly, seeking the deepest part of the pool, to lie on the bottom with his mouth open. Then he was on his side, dazed and weary, and the broken-quicksilvery surface of the pool was becoming whiter. He tried to swim away, but the water was too thick-heavy; and after a dozen sinuations it became solid. His head was out of water. A shock passed through him as he tried to breathe. He lay there, held by line taut over the fisherman's shoulder. He felt himself being drawn along just under the surface, and only then did he see his enemy—flattened, tremulant-spreading image of the fisherman. A new power of fear broke in the darkness of his lost self. When it saw the tailer coming down to it, the surface of the water was lashed by the desperately scattered self. The weight of the body falling over backwards struck the taut line; the tail-fin was split. The gut broke just above the hook, where it had been frayed on the rock. Salar saw himself winking down into the pool, and he lay there, scattered about himself and unable to move away, his tail curved round a stone, feeling only a distorted head joined to the immovable riverbed.

Discussion

    a. What details show that the author has closely observed the life of a salmon?

    b. Prepare a class debate on the topic: *Fishing is a cruel blood sport and should be abolished.*

Use Your Imagination

    a. Imagine yourself as an animal being chased or caught by a human. (See *Reynard the Fox* for an example in verse.)

    b. Which animal do you fear most? Imagine you are being chased by it, or them.

READING LISTS

LEGENDARY HEROES

Dragon Slayer, (Beowulf the Warrior), R. Sutcliff
Grettir the Strong, A. French
Havelock the Dane, K. Crossley-Holland
Heroes of British Isles, B. L. Picard
Heroes of Greece and Rome, R. L. Green
Heroes of the Kalevala, B. Deutsch
Hound of Ulster, R. Sutcliff
King Arthur and Knights of Round Table, R. L. Green
King Horn, K. Crossley-Holland
Knights of the Golden Table, E. M. Almedingen
Legend of El Cid, R. C. Goldston
Siege and Fall of Troy, Robert Graves
The Ivory Horn, Ian Serraillier

CRIMINAL HEROES

Adventures of Robin Hood, R. L. Green
Chronicles of Robin Hood, R. Sutcliff
More News from Sherwood, D. Suddaby
Robin Hood's Masterstroke, D. Suddaby

MONSTERS

A Book of Dragons, R. Manning-Saunders
A Book of Giants, R. Manning-Saunders
First Men on the Moon, H. G. Wells
My Friend Mr Leakey, J. B. S. Haldane
The Day of the Triffids, John Wyndham
The Dragon of the Hill, J. Gard
The Kraken Wakes, John Wyndham
The War of the Worlds, H. G. Wells

FIRE

Ash Road, Ivan Southall
Hiroshima, John Hersey
The Chrysalids, John Wyndham
The Day of the Bomb, K. Bruckner

FLOOD

Flood Warning, Paul Berna
Ice Cold River, Ruth France
Noah's Flood (Chester Miracle Cycle)
Play of Noah and Sons (Townley Cycle)
The Great Gale, H. Burton

ANIMAL FABLES

Fables From Aesop, J. Reeves
La Fontaine's Fables, M. Moore
Listen and I'll Tell You, E. Rorel
The Tiger's Whisker, H. Courlander
Twenty-five Fables, N. Montgomerie

ANIMAL SATIRES

Animal Farm, George Orwell
Stuart Little, E. B. White
The Animal's Conference, E. Kastner
The Wind in the Willows, K. Grahame

INDEX AND PRONUNCIATION GUIDE

Bold figures indicate extended references

THE GREEK GODS

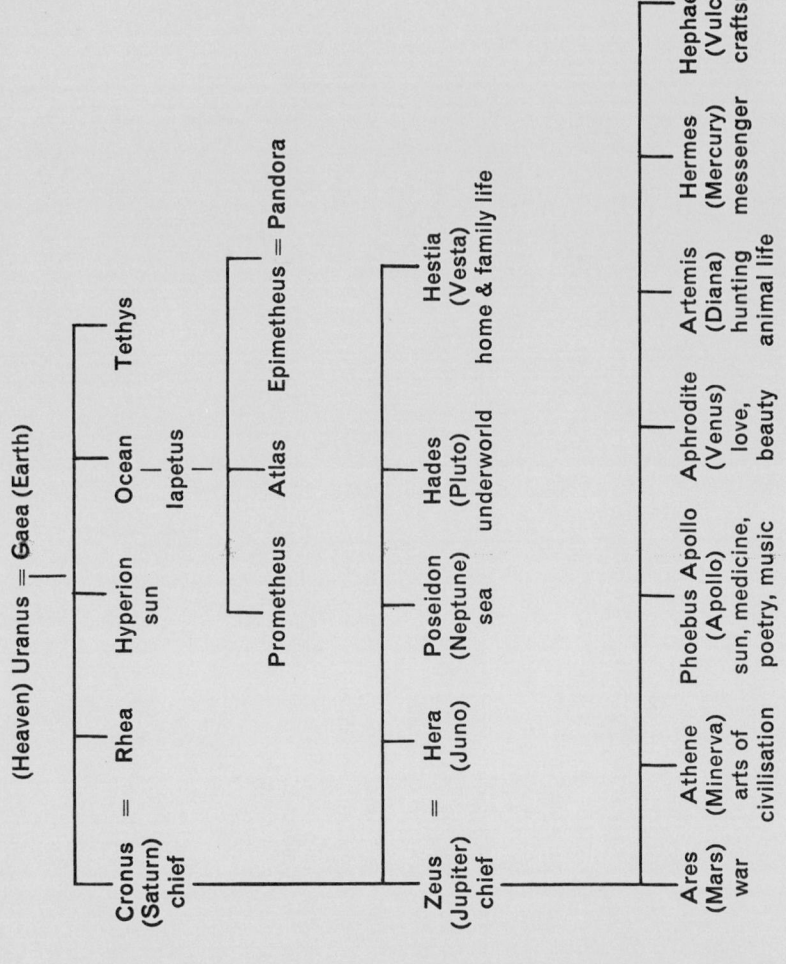

TITANS

(Heaven) Uranus = Gaea (Earth)

Cronus (Saturn) chief = Rhea

Hyperion sun

Ocean = Tethys

Iapetus

Prometheus   Atlas   Epimetheus = Pandora

OLYMPIANS

Zeus (Jupiter) chief = Hera (Juno)

Poseidon (Neptune) sea

Hades (Pluto) underworld

Hestia (Vesta) home & family life

Ares (Mars) war

Athene (Minerva) arts of civilisation

Phoebus Apollo (Apollo) sun, medicine, poetry, music

Aphrodite (Venus) love, beauty

Artemis (Diana) hunting animal life

Hermes (Mercury) messenger

Hephaestus (Vulcan) craftsman